Spirit Is Calling

Leela

Spirit Is Calling

•

A DAILY JOURNAL

Chris Michaels
Edward Viljoen

Awakening World Enterprises
Kansas City, Missouri

Awakening World Enterprises
1621 West Fiftieth Street
Kansas City, Missouri 64112

Printed in the United States of America.
Published November 2007

ISBN 0-974226-1-4
Library of Congress Control Number 2003111103

Design by Randall Friesen

*This journal is dedicated to all spiritual seekers
who are looking for answers deep within themselves.
Trust your intuition. Follow your heart.
It will lead to your destiny.*

*With heartfelt thanks to
Randall Friesen,
Tara Treasurfield,
Donna Lovell.*

This Is It!
Activating Spirituality
In Your Life

Spirituality is oftentimes thought of as a way of life. For it to be a way of life, though, it has to be more than something you think about; it has to be something you do. Most people, however, cannot drop out of their lives to focus exclusively on spiritual matters. But they can—with a little planning—take a few minutes a day to read an idea and write a few thoughts about it.

To truly activate spirituality in your life, the message, practice, and values of spirituality have to go beyond the weekly church, temple, or community experience and find their way into your awareness at home, at work, at play, in relationships…everywhere. *Spirit Is Calling*, an interactive journal, will help you do exactly that. It is designed to make the process accessible, even easy, so that giving your attention to your spiritual life is not cumbersome or unworkable. This can be it! Your adventure in spirituality can begin the moment you open this journal and start recording your thoughts.

Each daily entry features a spiritual value and invites you to set down your own thoughts about the value. The journal is organized into themes such as love, transformation, compassion, community, intuition, healing, service, prosperity, honesty, creativity, and joy.

At the end of the year, you will have given yourself an opportunity to discover what you think about spiritual values. That's actually the easy part. It gets interesting when you start to notice how this process affects your life. You'll be glad you decided to take time out for self-discovery and spiritual reflection.

This is your opportunity start again. Every New Yea presents an opportunity t set a new course for your life. Som people start the new year with reso lutions that last a few weeks months. As their lives continue pa the first days and weeks of the yea they slowly slip back into the pos tion they found themselves in at th end of the previous year.

To go the whole way with change and to truly activate spirituality in your life, it may take more than one solitary resolution. Rather than depend on one moment of decision to be renewed, you could support yourself by taking a moment each day this week, and the next week, and the week after that, until at last you find yourself at the end of a whole year of spiritually-focused living.

You don't have to do it all at once. Taking one day at a time, you can set an intention that steadily leads you into a deeper experience of your spiritual life. For example, use the space for "Notes" on this page today to write down what a renewed life might look like for you.

There c
can mai
truth...
way, c
Gauta

As you begin this journey of activating spirituality in your daily life, you will have the opportunity to practice mindfulness. You will become aware of your thoughts and actions different areas of your life as a result of this commitment to living spiritually-principled life. By taking time every day to reflect on your life, you will begin to notice how your actions, thoughts, and feelings tell the story of what you value.

What do you hope to accomplish as a result of this year-long practice of activating spirituality in your life?

SACRED SPACE

Sacred space is a term with many meanings. Most commonly, it refers to an environment that is being prepared for devotional activity. The preparation might include activities such as cleaning, clearing clutter and distraction, lighting candles, decorating, and so on. The idea is that our environment can affect our state of mind.

Sacred space can also describe the state of your mind when it is prepared for devotional activity. Sometimes circumstances prevent us from being in the perfect place for journaling, reflection, or prayer. It is at those times that we can create a sacred space within our minds by clearing clutter, slowing down, or listening to music that inspires peace.

How do you create sacred space within and around you for your daily journal practice?

NOTES

INSPIRATION
FOR TODAY
*Your sacred space is where
you can find yourself again
and again.*
Joseph Campbell

DAILY DEVOTIONAL

NOTES

Daily practice has an advantage over sporadic practice, in that regular attention to your spiritual life builds a rhythm in your awareness. This rhythm allows deeper insights emerge that are not possible with random program. This journal presents one of many possible devotional activities that might use to establish a regular daily rhythm introspection.

Take time each to read these journal entries and record your reflections or responses. The idea to insert spiritual values into your awareness daily basis, and thereby allow to influence your choices activities.

INSPIRATION
FOR TODAY
In the absence of clearly-defined goals, we become strangely loyal to performing daily trivia until ultimately we become enslaved by it."
Robert Heinlein

Imagine what might be released your life if every single day devoted some time to explore your inner life.

Since beginning this practice have you become aware of?

ALONE WITH SPIRIT

In our fast-paced society, multi tasking has become a standard survival strategy. It seems we have to know how to do many things at once: drive a complex vehicle, retrieve a phone number, navigate safely through traffic, and engage in an important conversation.

Many people make themselves available to this divided state of mind by having a cell phone in vibrate mode nearby at all times, even in theaters and museums. They have email alerts, voice mail, text messaging, as well as a constant stream of advertising images flooding in every second.

In your daily journal practice, consider giving yourself the luxurious experience of being undivided for ten or twenty minutes. Turn off all devices and put yourself somewhere that offers very little sensory stimulation. Explore what being "Alone With Spirit" might mean to you.

NOTES

_____

_____

_____

_____

_____

INSPIRATION
FOR TODAY
*Talking comes by nature,
silence by wisdom*
Proverb

_____

_____

_____

_____

_____

_____

_____

_____

_____

_____

January 6
SPIRITUAL PRACTICE

NOTES

_____

_____

_____

_____

_____

_____

_____

_____

_____

_____

_____

_____

_____

_____

_____

One meaning of the word "practice" is the focused repetition and effort applied to an activity for the purpose of becoming masterful in that activity. Practice creates familiarity with the activity and allows weaknesses and inconsistencies in technique to emerge so that they can be improved and adjusted if necessary.

INSPIRATION
FOR TODAY
The soul, like the body, accepts by practice whatever habit one wishes it to contact.
Socrates

Some days, practicing being still and writing in your journal may feel easier than others. There may be some days when you do better than others, or times when you know instinctively that you need a break.

Setting too high a standard or too rigid a schedule are ways of sabotaging your commitment to have a vibrant personal practice.

What adjustments, if any, do you need to make to your commitment to daily spiritual practice that will support your success?

WE ARE ONE

Science tells us that everything is composed of energy in some shape or form. This energy, present throughout the universe, shows up in an infinite variety of forms. From galaxies to planets, from human bodies to red roses, everything is made of energy.

This energy is *one*. Though it takes the form of many things, it exists as unity. It lives through whatever form it creates, expressing its variety and uniqueness. *You are that energy*!

You are a point of consciousness in an infinite universe that knows itself as *One*.

NOTES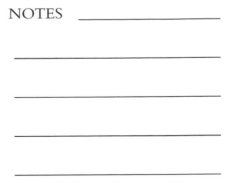

INSPIRATION
FOR TODAY
The Ultimate Cause back of all things must be One, since Life cannot be divided against Itself. The Infinite must be One, since there could not be two Infinite Beings.
Ernest Holmes

I AM PRESENT

I bought a raffle ticket recently, and printed on the back was the phrase, "Does not have to be present to win." This may be true to win a raffle, but it's certainly not true in life.

With all of life's distractions, staying present is sometimes the most difficult thing to do. Multi-tasking is the nation's new pastime and what many employers now expect from their workers.

To relieve the stress of modern life, practice being fully present. Give your full attention to one thing at a time. Be present!

INSPIRATION
FOR TODAY
This is what we all really want, what our heart wants, what our soul wants— this space just to be.
John Welwood, Ph.D.

NAMASTE

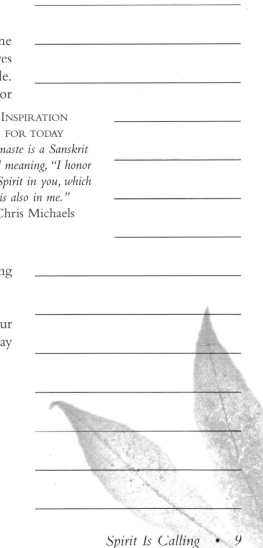

Namaste is a greeting that recognizes all beings as sacred and honorable. It acknowledges the *one Spirit* that lives and expresses itself in each of us.

Practice seeing God in everyone you meet this week. Lift your eyes to the "higher view" of people. Resist judging them as likable or unlikable personalities. See them for who they truly are—God incarnate.

Make a list of people who are easy for you to recognize as God incarnate. Now make a list of people you have a hard time seeing in this light.

Say a prayer of forgiveness for your lack of vision, and ask that you may see them as God does.

NOTES

INSPIRATION
FOR TODAY
Namaste is a Sanskrit word meaning, "I honor the Spirit in you, which is also in me."
Chris Michaels

GIFTS

There is only *one* Giver; God, the Creator and Sustainer of all life in the universe. All gifts and talents come directly from that One Source. Therefore, recognizing other peoples' gifts is really recognizing God in them. It is seeing the good that God has placed there.

Seeing the gifts that you bring to life is also seeing the good that God has given you. It bears witness to the generosity of your Creator and acknowledges graciously the good you take for granted every day.

INSPIRATION
FOR TODAY
Every good gift and every perfect gift is from above.
Bible, James 1:17
American Standard

Look for the good in yourself first and then in others. Dismiss and forgive as quickly as possible the things you judge as flawed or bad. Whatever you look for in others tends to rise to the surface. When you recognize the good in others, you greet God daily.

RIGHT SPEAKING

How many times have you said something that you later wish you hadn't? How many people have been hurt by your words? How often have you wished you could take them back?

Once spoken, our words travel far. They either uplift and inspire others or bring them despair and pain. The spoken word is powerful. It can make or break another person.

INSPIRATION
FOR TODAY
The voice is a second face.
Gerard Bauer

You hold that power in your mouth each day. What you say to yourself determines your attitude. What you say to children decides their self-esteem. What you say to others determines who stays in your life and who goes.

In this journal, write something you said today that made you feel proud. Now write something you said that had the opposite effect. What can you do tomorrow to reverse the negative impact of your words? Vow to do it.

January 12

NO CHANCE MEETINGS

In a universe governed by Perfect Intelligence, there can be no errors, mistakes, or coincidences. Everything is synchronized for our greater good, whether we are aware of it or not.

We look too closely and judge too quickly. We frivolously believe in luck, fate, and chance when there are no such powers in our lives.

If I'd gotten the job I wanted at Montgomery Ward, I suppose I would never have left Illinois.
Ronald Reagan

Every person you meet has something of value to bring to your life and vice versa. No matter how long they stay in your life, recognize their entrance as a divine event, perfectly synchronized by a Master Mind. With every person who crosses your path, make it your intention to leave them better than you found them.

When things don't go your way, trust there is a "Higher Way" that you may not be able to see right now.

SPIRITUAL BEINGS

You are not your body, nor does your value come from the size, shape or age of it. You are not your resume, assets or accomplishments. You are a spiritual being, not a human body with a crossed-off list of things to do.

All of your value comes from what you have on the inside, not what is visible on the outside. Your spirit is eternal. It grows in wisdom but does not age. It lives through your body, but is not limited by it. It cloaks itself in whatever kind of body best serves its spiritual growth. And it stays in one place only long enough to gather the experience necessary to expand and flourish.

Begin seeing yourself as a spiritual being on a journey of discovery. Let go of old identifications and definitions.

NOTES

INSPIRATION
FOR TODAY
You are a spiritual being created by God, living in a universe governed by spiritual Law. You are a unique creation of a Perfect Intelligence and your life is a once-in-a-lifetime opportunity to express who you are!
Chris Michaels
Your Soul's Assignment

January 14
GIVING

Activating spirituality in your finances means to be committed to seeing your finances from a spiritual perspective. Focusing today on "giving," make an honest assessment of the role giving plays in your life. What are your attitudes about giving? Make an inventory of where and how much you are giving (to others or to organizations) and notice the feelings associated with your giving. If you are not currently giving financially, use today's entry to explore your reasons.

INSPIRATION
FOR TODAY
No one has ever become
poor by giving.
Anne Frank

RECEIVING

Some people have no difficulty giving. It is a joyful activity for them. Some people, however well they give, have difficulty receiving. Sometimes it is because the act of receiving may have associations that cause them to feel uncomfortable. Perhaps they have learned that if they receive something they have an obligation to compensate or return a gift. Or maybe receiving is associated with being weak. Or maybe receiving carries with it a fear of being manipulated or obliged.

What is your relationship to receiving? What would it be like today to accept everything and anything that was given to you with nothing more than "Thank You" given in return?

INSPIRATION
FOR TODAY
*Human life runs its course
in the metamorphosis
between receiving
and giving.*
Goethe

January 16
ASKING

NOTES

S ome people have no difficulty asking for what they need. Others have been taught to manage without asking, or to wait until help is offered. Some have an idea that asking imposes unwelcome obligation on others, or that asking is a sign of weakness. Asking may even evoke feelings of greed or unworthiness, or may be a sign of poor behavior.

INSPIRATION
FOR TODAY
*He who is afraid of asking
is ashamed of learning.*
Danish Proverb

Today's assignment is to practice asking. Write down everything you have ever wanted. Do this for the purpose of observing your feelings and thoughts as you engage in the exercise. You don't have to do anything with the list; just notice the feelings you have about it.

CIRCULATION

S tanding water is prone to stagnation. Circulating water brings freshness and vitality. Applying this metaphor of water to your life, imagine that the water is any good thing you want to experience. For example, love, friendship, time, creativity.

Now consider this: you don't create love, friendship or whatever it is you are thinking of. Like the water, these things have their origin in creation itself. You can't create any more of these things; however, you have some control over the degree of flow.

Think of love flowing in only one direction as having the same effect as water flowing into one location, without any outlet. Thinking specifically about money today, describe the balance between giving and receiving in your life.

NOTES

INSPIRATION
FOR TODAY

If you help others you will be helped, perhaps tomorrow, perhaps in one hundred years, but you will be helped. Nature must pay off the debt... it is a mathematical law and all life is mathematics.
Gurdjieff

INTEGRITY

NOTES

Integrity describes a state of harmony, as in, for example, harmony between words and actions. In a simple form, integrity means keeping promises or following through with commitments and being prompt about making amends when promises and commitments can no longer be kept.

Establishing financial integrity is an example of how to maintain an open "flow." For some people, the first step towards financial integrity is to become aware of their financial status by bringing order into matters such as their checkbook records, bill payment schedules, money owed or owing.

INSPIRATION
FOR TODAY
Integrity is doing the right thing, even if nobody is watching.
Unknown

HARMONY

Seeing your finances from a spiritual perspective can also mean viewing money in a spiritual light. Instead of working to make money, or instead of seeing money as the pathway to harmony and security, you could begin to think of money as one of the commodities Spirit uses to keep everything flowing harmoniously.

In the idioms of our language, many negative ideas about money are commonplace. Money is considered by some to be dirty, the root of evil, corrupt and dangerous.

Look for idioms about money that describe it in affirmative ways. You may need to create some of your own new sayings to describe money in a harmonious way.

NOTES

INSPIRATION
FOR TODAY
Happiness is not in the mere possession of money; it lies in the joy of achievement, in the thrill of creative effort.
Franklin D. Roosevelt

PROSPERITY

Dr. Paul Ray, author of *The Cultural Creatives,* was recently asked how we can live prosperously and still honor the lives of all six billion people on our planet. Can this world sustain all people living prosperously? His response was, "Yes, as long as we expand our definition of prosperity."

INSPIRATION
FOR TODAY
When prosperity comes, do not use all of it.
Confucius

Prosperity is more than having enough money. Sometimes, having more money may not create greater prosperity for your life. Living an abundant life is really about having enough freedom. It is not necessarily about the "quantity of stuff." It's about quality of life.

With this in mind, consider that you define what prosperity is. Your definition may be different from every other definition you have heard. People live prosperously at all levels of income because prosperity is not about money; it's about freedom and love.

What does prosperity mean to you?

LOVING MY BODY

By now, most of us have heard the term, "use it or lose it" in reference to our bodies. And yet we still try to ignore the fact that our bodies need regular exercise in order to stay healthy. We find all kinds of excuses why we can't find the time to go to the gym or take a few extra minutes in the morning to stretch and do yoga.

The truth is that we take good care of what we love the most. We put fine china in the cabinet where it is safe. We wash and detail the car. We make sure our loved ones buckle up when they get in the car.

Treat your body as if you *love* it. Take time out of your busy day to give it what it needs: good food and regular exercise. And when you catch your reflection in the mirror, give yourself a wink and say, "You are fabulous!"

NOTES

_____

_____

_____

_____

_____

INSPIRATION
FOR TODAY
*What we use grows
stronger; what we ignore
becomes weaker and begins
to diminish until finally
it has no energy to
sustain itself.*
Dennis Merritt Jones
The Art of Being

_____

_____

_____

_____

_____

_____

January 22

EXAMINING BELIEFS

Every thought has a biological response. Every mood either enhances or inhibits your health. Your attitude produces a corresponding reaction in your body.

Maintaining a healthy body isn't just about what kind of food you eat, or whether you get regular exercise. Equally important is what you think about on a regular basis.

INSPIRATION
FOR TODAY

*...your health is the sum
total of all the impulses,
positive and negative,
emanating from your
consciousness.
You are what you think.*
Deepak Chopra

Statistics show that happy people tend to be healthier people. People who have a positive attitude heal faster than others.

If you really want to be healthy, find out what brings you happiness, then do it. Joy is the essential ingredient for health.

What have you done today that was fun? What made you laugh? Who did you see today that you love?

Filling your life with love and joy is the most productive thing you can do to create health.

EMOTIONALLY PRESENT

Many people find it diffi-cult to express them-selves emotionally. Our society does not condition us to do so. In fact, it teaches us to repress our emotions, not express them.

However, we have been designed by our Creator to experience strong emotions. Without passion and joy, life would be meaningless.

Being present emotional-ly means giving yourself permission to feel any particular way, without judgment or condemna-tion.

I saw an interview on television of a woman who sur-vived a plane crash, while her family perished. She talked about how angry she was with God and how inappropriate she thought her anger was. After much soul search-ing, she realized it was okay to be angry with God. Giving herself permission to feel any emotion, without judgment led her back to health and happiness.

Feel your feelings! Don't judge them—just let them come and go, as they are supposed to.

NOTES

INSPIRATION FOR TODAY

You can't give something you don't have. You can't be emotionally present with someone else if you're not there for yourself.
Chris Michaels

HEALTHY CHOICES

There is a guiding Force within that will lead you directly to healthy choices. It knows exactly what is necessary to maintain optimum health. If you will listen closely, this Higher Power will tell you everything you need to know.

Inside our bodies is the Intelligence that designed them. It is not stationary. It is at work all of the time doing what is necessary to sustain our bodies. You are its partner. The choices you make either support or inhibit its movement.

INSPIRATION FOR TODAY

What you're looking for is not in the refrigerator. It's in you, deep inside, in your connection to a Higher Power and a higher purpose.

Victoria Moran
Fat, Broke & Lonely No More

Not only does making healthy choices create a healthier body, it's also the best thing you can do to increase self-esteem. Witnessing yourself making the higher choice builds regard and respect. That in turn causes feelings of worth and value.

Everything begins with your choice. You are not a victim of circumstances. You are a powerful being making conscious choices.

NEW PRACTICES

There will never come a time in your life when you can say, "I am done now." We are all a "work-in-progress."

Knowing this can set you free of comparison to others. We're all on different paths, making unique choices, learning powerful truths. Your soul is unfolding and transforming itself through love and wisdom. This is a process, not a destination.

In the process of the soul's unfolding, it's best to take special care of its needs. Everything responds to loving attention, including your soul's growth.

Light a candle today as an act of mindfulness. Watch the flame burn, remembering that it's fluid and spontaneous, just as you are. Say a prayer. Make a commitment.

Create a new practice that honors your soul, one that recognizes the journey and celebrates your successes.

NOTES

INSPIRATION
FOR TODAY
*Our work in psychology
would change remarkably if
we thought about it as
ongoing care rather than as
the quest for a cure.*
Thomas Moore
Care of the Soul

VITALITY

_____

_____

_____

_____

_____

_____

_____

_____

_____

_____

_____

_____

_____

_____

_____

_____

**INSPIRATION
FOR TODAY**
*When you cease to
make a contribution,
you begin to die.*
Eleanor Roosevelt

E ach of us needs to know that what we contribute to life makes a difference in some way. We need to feel as though we're a vital part of life and that what we do matters on some scale. This is an important part of maintaining mental and psychological health.

It doesn't matter whether you are a bread-maker or a brain surgeon. What matters is that you enjoy what you do and leave work with a sense of accomplishment.

Feeling vital is important to the soul and body. Exercise and good food create a vital body. But, the soul needs something it can give to life that will make things better for someone else. To be vital, it needs to be engaged in life and to make a contribution.

What is your contribution? What do you do that makes a difference? What makes you feel vital?

SPIRITUAL HEALTH

Your reality is created by focusing your attention. What you give your attention to expands in your world of experience.

Hate-filled people give a great deal of attention to what they hate. They think about all of the injustice in the world and focus on their resentments. Loving people, on the other hand, give their attention to what they love the most in life. They focus on the people they love, the satisfaction they gain from their work and the gratitude they feel for life.

Spiritual health is created by focusing your attention on all that is good and well in your life. It comes to the mind, body and spirit of the person who knows the power of their thought.

Think about what you love today. Focus your mind on all that is well. Feel the sense of gratitude that comes from accepting so many blessings.

INSPIRATION FOR TODAY

What you pay attention to grows. If your attention is attracted to negative situations and emotions, then they will grow in your awareness.
Deepak Chopra

NOTES

January 28
MY GIFTS

What value do you bring to the world? Some people find it easier to list their faults than to list their value. Others underestimate themselves by overlooking skills and talents they consider to be ordinary. Nevertheless, everyone excels at something and everyone loves doing something.

FOR TODAY
When I stand before God at the end of my life, I would hope that I would not have a single bit of talent left, and could say, "I used everything you gave me."
Erma Bombeck

Here is an effective method for exploring your gifts and talents. Ask a good friend to describe what your gifts are, and write them down without editing. When your friend is done, try asking an additional question: "What am I doing when I am most happy?"

Your friend's answers may surprise you.

28 • *Spirit Is Calling*

NURTURING MYSELF

Do you treat yourself well? Do you take vacations? Do you have down-time? Do you take personal time in which you are at liberty to do anything or nothing? Do you give yourself adequate sleep? Do you exercise your body and feed it nutritious food? Do you take time to indulge in the things you love doing and to be with the people you love being with?

What does nurturing yourself mean to you and how can you do more of it?

NOTES

INSPIRATION
FOR TODAY
*Our remedies oft in our-
selves do lie; Which we
ascribe to heaven.*
Shakespeare

APPRECIATING ME

NOTES

_____

_____

_____

_____

_____

_____

_____

_____

_____

_____

_____

_____

_____

_____

INSPIRATION
FOR TODAY
_We have to learn to be
our own best friends
because we fall too easily
into the trap of being our
own worst enemies._
Roderick Thorp

One of the meanings of the word "appreciate" is to raise in value. That which is without value is typically not cherished. It doesn't take much for something to become valuable—only a decision. Someone decides what is valuable to them, and then that item receives their loving attention. They raise that item's value. Perhaps they protect it or grant it favored status in their home or on their schedule.

What decisions do you need to make to raise your value in your own estimation?

SPIRIT LIVES IN ME

"Omnipresent" is a wonderful word used to describe the "everywhere-presentness" of Spirit. It means that in every spot of creation (without exception), Spirit is present. Some people use the word "life" as a synonym for Spirit and say that Life is everywhere present. It means the same thing. Using both terms, you might want to consider this idea, that Spirit lives everywhere...and of course, that means in you, too.

Taking it further, you might say something like this: "The life I am living is Spirit's life." Ideas like these take time to contemplate.

What comes to mind when you say, "The life I am living is Spirit's life"? What questions arise for you?

NOTES

INSPIRATION
FOR TODAY
We are not human beings on a spiritual journey. We are spiritual beings on a human journey.
Stephen R. Covey

February 1
BEAUTY

"Beauty is in the eye of the beholder" is a phrase that is well known to the extent that its wisdom can be overlooked. Rephrased it says, "What you perceive to be beautiful is uniquely your experience and may or may not match any other person's perception or definition of beauty."

When you take time to listen to your own wisdom, what do you behold in yourself to be beautiful? Regardless of what other people consider to be beautiful, what in you do you consider beautiful?

INSPIRATION
FOR TODAY
*Beauty is not in the face;
beauty is a light
in the heart.*
Kahlil Gibran

It may be helpful to consider this definition of beauty: the quality present in a thing or person that gives intense pleasure or deep satisfaction to the mind.

THE IDEAL ME

How many images and messages does the average person receive about the ideal human being? Probably too many to be able to accurately estimate. Somewhere among these mental pictures is your own "ideal you."

Without referring to the perfection of the advertising world, how would you describe the ideal you? How does the ideal you feel and look? What hobby does the ideal you participate in?

Ask yourself, "Who and what is the ideal me?" Then sit quietly and let the answers emerge.

NOTES

INSPIRATION
FOR TODAY
*You can tell the ideals
of a nation by its
advertisements.*
Norman Douglas

LOVING MYSELF

Loving yourself may be both the most beneficial and the most challenging project you ever attempted because of how well you know yourself. You are aware of your weaknesses in a way that no other person is. With this in mind, your practice of self love might need to be approached with a forgiving disposition.

INSPIRATION
FOR TODAY
To love oneself is the beginning of a life-long romance
Oscar Wilde

You're also aware of what brings you peace and pleasure like no other person is, so loving yourself is about finding ways to bring pleasure and peace into your life.

What one thing can you do today that will show self love?

THE GIFTS OF OTHERS

Everyone has something unique and valuable to bring to life. Even the people we judge as wounded or evil serve as examples to others of what choices not to make.

Every person you meet has something valuable to bring to your life. When you go about the business of everyday living, expect everyone you meet to prosper your life. Expect other people to like you. Assume that you will like them. See the good in others and it will rise to the surface to greet you.

What gifts did you see today that others gave you?

NOTES

INSPIRATION
FOR TODAY
*Every person you meet is
a new opportunity to bless
your life. The question is:
Are you ready to receive
the blessing?*
Chris Michaels

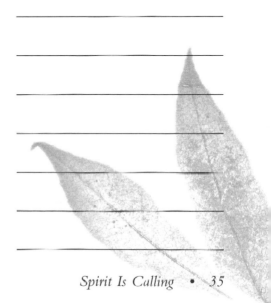

February 5

NURTURING OTHERS

Every vehicle has blind spots that obstruct the driver's view. That same truth applies to each of us. We all have our own blind spots, areas of our lives that we just can't figure out.

Ironically, it's easy to see where other people's blind spots are. It's easy to determine what they should do to improve their lives. And many times we're quite eager to tell them. However, that's not what people really need from us. They don't need us to tell them what to do. They don't need our judgment or criticism. What they really need is our love and compassion.

They need what you need when you struggle with your own issues. They need understanding, comfort and nurturing. More than your advice, they need your love and acceptance.

Who is in your life today that could use some support? What can you do to nurture them?

APPRECIATING OTHERS

After being together for ten years, my sweetheart and I did not know what to do for Valentine's Day. Should we get each other another meaningless card and go out to dinner, as we'd done every year for the last decade?

With the date quickly approaching, a new idea came to mind. Why not stay at home, make a wonderful dinner-for-two and read each other a love letter?

The evening turned out to be the most meaningful Valentine's Day we had ever shared. We said things in our letters to each other that were not only true, but really beautiful and kind.

All of the other Valentine's Day cards I had received over the years got tossed in the trash a few days later. But the letters we wrote to each other remain in a cherished place in our home forevermore.

What kindness have you left unspoken? What do you appreciate in your friends or family that you've never verbalized? What are you waiting for?

NOTES

INSPIRATION
FOR TODAY
*We have a great deal
more kindness than
is ever spoken.*
Ralph Waldo Emerson,
Essay on Friendship

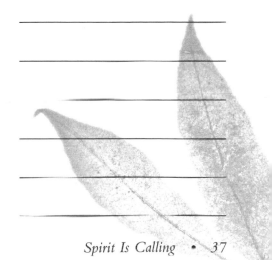

February 7

SPIRIT LIVES
THROUGH OTHERS

The people you attract into your life do not come by mistake or error. Your friends are a gift from God. They come to support your spiritual growth and challenge you to be more than you would be without them around to hold you accountable. They mirror your beliefs and present you with opportunities to see God as them.

INSPIRATION
FOR TODAY
My friends have come to me unsought. The great God gave them to me.
Ralph Waldo Emerson

Some examples of God-qualities might include love, joy, ease, peace, courage, authority, harmony, wholeness, etc.

What God-qualities do you see in your closest friend? What God-qualities do you see in yourself?

THE BEAUTY OF OTHERS

We have been made by our Creator to live as individuals—each one of us bringing something uniquely beautiful to life.

Never try to imitate others. Be true to the beauty that lies inside *you*! Never conform to what others expect just to appease them. Don't waste precious time trying to force your truth on others. Respect your differences and learn to see the beauty of God's diversity.

INSPIRATION
FOR TODAY

Love one another, but make not a bond of love: Let it rather be a moving sea between the shores of your souls. Fill each other's cup but drink not from the same cup. Give one another of your bread but eat not from the same loaf. Sing and dance together and be joyous, but let each of you be alone, even as the strings of a lute are alone though they quiver with the same music.
Kahlil Gibran

NOTES

THE IDEAL HUMAN

NOTES _____

_____

_____

_____

_____

_____

_____

_____

_____

_____

_____

_____

_____

_____

_____

_____

D eep inside your soul is the seed of your perfection, placed there by God. As you discover the richness that lies inside of you, change begins to show up in your outer world. What was acceptable before is no longer good enough.

Recognize this change for what it is: God demanding to be let out. Now is the time to follow your best ideas. Listen to your heart. Respect your intuitions.

INSPIRATION
FOR TODAY
_We are in the midst
of a massive up-welling of
human potential, creativity,
anger and frustration.
We are confused and
reactionary, yet bursting
with new capacities..._
just like a newborn child.
Barbara Marx Hubbard
Conscious Evolution

LOVING OTHERS

When you love someone, you take a risk. They may not be able to love you in return. They may not treat you well or be true. They may pass away. They may get sick. There are a thousand different risks you take every day when you love other people. But the risks are worth taking when so much is gained in return.

We experience God's love through others. We practice acceptance, compassion and tolerance in our relationships with other people. They provide us with opportunities to grow spiritually and prepare us to accept an even greater love—the perfect, eternal, unconditional love of God.

What have you learned about yourself by loving others? How have you grown in your understanding of compassion and acceptance?

NOTES

INSPIRATION FOR TODAY

To open your heart and give love to another person is risky. But an open heart is the only way to really experience God.
Chris Michaels

February 11
THE GIFTS OF SPIRIT

What are the gifts of the Spirit? Whatever they are, they must be universal, permanent, eternal, uncaused, and unconditioned.

Universal: whatever is true of the Universe must also be true of the individual who is some part of the Universe. Permanent: lasting without vital change. Eternal: without beginning or ending, existing outside of time—continuing without interruption—forever true and changeless. Uncaused: having no apparent reason for being. Unconditioned: not dependent on any prerequisite or condition.

What in you is universal, permanent, eternal, uncaused and unconditional?

INSPIRATION
FOR TODAY
*Love is something eternal;
the aspect may change, but
not the essence.*
Vincent van Gogh

42 • Spirit Is Calling

LONGING FOR DIVINITY

Consider this: many people embark on a journey of spiritual exploration because they have a longing to be loved in a way that no human being can love. Their journey may bring them face to face with divine acceptance, which is the idea that Spirit embraces all beings, all the time.

And then they face larger questions…can I love like that, too? What is God's love like, and can I love that way?

NOTES _____

_____

_____

_____

_____

**INSPIRATION
FOR TODAY**

*Feeling and longing are the
motive forces behind all
human endeavor and
human creations.*
Albert Einstein

_____

_____

_____

_____

_____

_____

_____

_____

_____

APPRECIATING LIFE

NOTES

Today, consider loving what Creation has produced. Begin to watch life around you as an experiment in appreciating its finest qualities. Watch creation today as if you are observing a performance on stage. Watch it as if you have been charged with giving it a score. Here's what you're looking for: elegant coincidences, unexpected shifts, patterns and beauty.

INSPIRATION
FOR TODAY
Gratitude is not only the greatest of virtues, but the parent of all others.
Cicero

At the end of the day, write a note of appreciation to Life, pointing out some of the finer moments from the day.

SPIRIT SURROUNDS ME

Try this: repeat to yourself as you progress through the day, "Spirit surrounds me." At the end of the day, make note of anything you notice as a result of this practice.

NOTES

INSPIRATION
FOR TODAY
*Nature is too thin a screen;
the glory of the
omnipresent God bursts
through everywhere.*
Ralph Waldo Emerson

DIVINE BEAUTY

Longing for divinity brings you inescapably into loving the way God loves: open heartedly, without reason or reward. To love this way, you have to see things and people as "beautiful," divinely beautiful—regardless of what they look like, or even what they are doing—to see their beauty because they are created by God...and attempt to really love that.

INSPIRATION
FOR TODAY
The best part of beauty is that which no picture can express.
Francis Bacon. Sr.

What is divine beauty to you?

UNCONDITIONAL LOVE

An example of loving with a condition is "I will love you if..." or "I will love you because..." or "I will love you when..." Thinking of someone in your life you love deeply, what, if any, are your conditions for loving them? What does it mean to love someone unconditionally? Is it possible? Have you experienced it?

NOTES

INSPIRATION
FOR TODAY
*The ultimate lesson
all of us have to learn is
unconditional love, which
includes not only others
but ourselves as well.*
Elisabeth Kubler-Ross

LOVING SPIRIT

NOTES

Think of Spirit as a synonym for Creation or Reality. Then, when you are loving Spirit, you can actually be loving Creation or loving Reality.

What things in Creation do you truly love? How do you feel, think, and act when you love them?

INSPIRATION
FOR TODAY
*Beer is proof
that God loves us and
wants us to be happy.*
Benjamin Franklin

CONSCIOUS ACTION

When we follow The Tao's advice, our actions become mindful and conscious. We contribute to the solution, instead of being part of the problem.

What does it mean to "work without working at"? What challenges are you dealing with today?

INSPIRATION FOR TODAY

Act without acting on. Work without working at. Enter bountifulness when it is still insufficiency. Answer with kindness when faced with hostility. Begin a difficult task in its easy stage because large problems grow from small ones. Begin a large task in its formative state because complex issues originate from simple ones. But beware of those who promise quick and easy solutions! Accept problems as challenges. In this way, the sage accomplishes great tasks without ever having to struggle with them.
The Tao Te Ching

February 19

GENTLE TOUCH

NOTES

You are surrounded by God's gentle embrace. The Great Lover is with you at all times, awaiting your growing awareness of its Presence.

Know that you are in the Presence of the Divine. Walk softly. Touch things and people in a gentle and respectful way. Be kind to yourself. Speak kindly of others. Look for beauty.

What did you see today that was beautiful? What touched your heart?

INSPIRATION
FOR TODAY
*May I walk with Beauty
before me.
May I walk with Beauty
behind me.
May I walk with Beauty
above me.
May I walk with Beauty
below me.
May I walk with Beauty
all around me.
As I walk the Beauty way.*
Navajo Prayer

FRIENDLY UNIVERSE

The word universe means "uni-verse," or "one song." It reminds us that the universe is *one* living organism, sustained by *one* intelligence.

The intelligence at the helm of our universe is God. Its desire for self-expression created, and now sustains, an infinitely expanding universe.

Jesus said, "It is the Father's pleasure to give," thus reminding us that it is God's nature to be kind and loving. Remember this truth as you go about the business of your day. There is nothing in the universe that wants to cause you harm or make you fail. All there is, is God.

The universe is friendly, and all is well!

NOTES

INSPIRATION FOR TODAY

Albert Einstein once said the most important question a human being can ask is, "Is the universe friendly?"

February 21
ATTITUDE MATTERS

NOTES

What you give your attention to creates a mental atmosphere around you that determines what is attracted into your experience. What you focus your attention on expands exponentially.

Fear attracts fearful people. Desperation attracts desperate people. Confidence and faith attract people who are strong and faithful. Your attitude (consciousness) is powerful.

INSPIRATION FOR TODAY

Today you are to identify yourself with the more abundant life, to think on those things which make for peace, to dwell on unity which underlies everything. Focus your inward vision on this indwelling harmony...
Ernest Holmes
This Thing Called You

Before you leave the house each day, say to yourself: "I have everything I need to be successful today. All of the power in the universe is on my side. Thank God I am alive."

HOLY GROUND

Since God is present in every location simultaneously, every place you stand is holy ground. You are always in the presence of Spirit.

Some psychologists say that we have a chronic sense of disconnection with life because we don't spend enough time touching the earth. We walk on carpeted floors, drive on paved roads and sleep on mattresses. Our bodies rarely touch the planet from which they were formed. We come from the earth and we need it to survive, not just physically, but emotionally and psychologically as well.

Go outdoors. Breathe the air. Touch the ground. Connect what is holy within you, with what is holy in the earth. Practice being in God's Presence.

NOTES

INSPIRATION
FOR TODAY
...the place on which you are standing is holy ground.
Exodus 3:5

RESPECTFULNESS

When you treat yourself with respect, you honor what God has created. When you treat others with respect, you recognize your Oneness with all people. When you treat your things with respect, you are able to see God in all things. When you treat the planet with respect, you recognize the Presence of the Holy Spirit.

INSPIRATION
FOR TODAY
R.E.S.P.E.C.T.—
find out what it
means to me.
Aretha Franklin

Never demand respect from others! Show respect for yourself—and you won't have to fight or argue to get others to respect you.

Give the very thing you want to receive in return. Respect others and they will show respect for you.

Have you disrespected yourself? Have you disrespected others? Have you disrespected the planet? What can you do to correct the situation?

EVERYTHING IS GOD

There is a Universal Energy out of which all things, including your body, are made. That Energy is perfect. It lives through and maintains the form of everything from a rock on the ground to the furthest star in the sky.

Every person is God (Energy & Intelligence) incarnate. Every thing is God, in form. That's why it's important to treat your possessions with respect and other people with love and compassion. You are immersed in God, like a fish in water. There's nowhere to escape Its loving embrace.

Look around. You'll see God in everything!

NOTES

INSPIRATION
FOR TODAY
If you can't see God in all things, then you can't see God in anything.
Bumper Sticker

February 25

THE NATURE OF NATURE

It is the nature of nature to transform. Not one thing in creation stands still. Not even a solid rock or a piece of steel. At the center of everything solid, there is movement. For some things in nature, the changes are clear and obvious: seasons, beginnings and endings, plants and flowers. For other things in nature, the change is spread over time and across many cycles. What starts as a stream eventually turns into a canyon. A wafer-thin seed turns into a redwood tree.

What in your life changes slowly and what changes quickly?

INSPIRATION
FOR TODAY
*Adapt or perish,
now as ever, is nature's
inexorable imperative.*
H.G. Wells

SIMPLE BEGINNINGS

Nature begins simply and as changes progress, the more complex are the results. A small seed hears some silent call to sprout and, drawing upon the universe of support around it in the dark soil, begins a journey of ever-increasing complexity. Over time it changes into something truly amazing.

Similarly, the process of learning a new skill or language begins slowly and simply. With the introduction of small pieces of information in a measured way, the student slowly begins to understand ideas and information far beyond the meaning of the individual words.

If you're starting something new, consider that your regular, consistent attention will yield something truly wonderful. It may be difficult to imagine what a practice of daily journaling will lead to, but consider that seed in you responding to a silent call to become something magnificent.

NOTES

INSPIRATION
FOR TODAY

Every contrivance of man, every tool, every instrument, every utensil, every article designed for use, of each and every kind, evolved from a very simple beginning.
Robert Collier

February 27

SPIRIT EXPRESSING

All transformation is Spirit expressing itself. What a glorious idea! There is no end to the possibilities. If divinity is infinite, endless, and unlimited, that would mean it is forever and ever changing from what it is today, to what it is tomorrow, and so on. That would suggest that life is a journey and not a destination.

INSPIRATION
FOR TODAY
The best day of your life is the one on which you decide your life is your own. No apologies or excuses. No one to lean on, rely on, or blame. The gift is yours—it is an amazing journey—and you alone are responsible for the quality of it.
Bob Maowad

If you started at the beginning of the year, this is the second month of activating spirituality in your life. What have you noticed? How have you changed?

CHANGE IS GOOD

It is curious that in a world of constant movement, where transformation is the norm, human beings long for that which does not change. Getting clearer on what is changeless and what changes is a helpful exercise in developing a healthy relationship with change.

In your opinion, what can you be certain is changeless, and what is changing right now? How do you feel about change?

NOTES

INSPIRATION
FOR TODAY
*Mad is the man
who is forever gritting his
teeth against that granite
block, complete and
changeless of the past.*
Antoine de
Saint-Exupery

February 29

LIFE IS A JOURNEY

Life is a journey that has no end destination. Perhaps there are moments of rest and regrouping. And yet every milestone on the path has endless potential and any number of next steps and new possible directions. The ever-changing landscape brings up questions like these: Would you stay on the current path? Will you forge a new path? What will you do if the path leads somewhere you weren't expecting?

INSPIRATION
FOR TODAY
*The path of least
resistance is what makes
rivers run crooked.*
Elbert Hubbard

I MAKE ALL THINGS

"Behold, I make all things new" is what God announced in the book of Revelations. It is the declaration of Life's tendency to change ceaselessly from what it *is* into what it is *becoming*. The former falls away and in its place is exactly what is necessary for the next phase of life. What else could it be?

Where in your life are you experiencing the rebirth of something?

NOTES

March 2
TRANSFORMATION

NOTES

We are all in some state of transformation. We are at different stages, moving at different speeds, transforming in different areas. It makes life very interesting. One person's career seems stable but her relationships are transforming as she begins to open her heart to a deep love. Another person's romantic life is solid, while changes in his family life initiate changes in finances. This variety gives us the opportunity to be patient with each other and to take turns leaning on each other and inspiring each other.

INSPIRATION
FOR TODAY
Without accepting the fact that everything changes, we cannot find perfect composure.
Shunryu Suzuki

Where are you changing and where are you stable?

PART OF THE WHOLE

Things are not as they appear. The universe has not been divided into parts. Life is like a holographic projection: the full picture can be seen in every part.

Though it appears that you are separate from everyone around you, the truth is that we are all *one*! On the soul level we are all interconnected and draw our existence from *one* Source.

Your life is part of a bigger picture. Your story is part of a bigger story. You have an important and significant role to play in the evolution of consciousness on planet earth.

How do you feel your *oneness* with Life/God? What happens when you feel alone and separate?

NOTES

INSPIRATION
FOR TODAY
*...everything in the universe
is part of a continuum.
Despite the apparent
separateness of things at the
explicate level, everything is
a seamless extension of
everything else...*
Michael Talbot
The Holographic Universe

NEW DISCOVERIES

Every day is a new opportunity to discover something new about life. Children know this. That's why they are so excited to begin a new day.

As adults, it's easy to lose touch with the excitement and enthusiasm of our youth. We struggle to keep it alive when we are bombarded with adult responsibilities and burdens. It's easy to fall into the trap of getting old and bitter.

By staying conscious to the wonders and mysteries of life, we prevent our fall into cynicism and bitterness. We must remind ourselves to do something new each day, take a risk, go somewhere different, try a new food. That's what keeps us young and alive.

What will you do today that you've never done before?

INSPIRATION
FOR TODAY
You are starting out on a great adventure, a wonderful journey. You are guided by love, inspired by truth, and your future will be what you make it.
Ernest Holmes
This Thing Called You

LEAVING MY FOOTPRINT

Being alive at this time in history is not an accident or fluke of nature. You were created by a perfect Intelligence that knows exactly what It is doing.

You are here now because the world has need of the gifts you brought here. You are here to make a difference. Your goal is to leave things better than you found them when you arrived.

Though it may seem that the small things we do, such as encouraging someone to pursue their dream, committing a random act of kindness, or designing a well-planted garden, don't really make a difference. They do. Every kind and loving act leaves a footprint behind for someone else to see and follow.

What legacy would you like to leave for the world?

NOTES

INSPIRATION FOR TODAY
You were created for a reason and with an intention. There's something you're supposed to be doing with your life that will make a difference to the world; something significant and powerful!
Chris Michaels
Your Soul's Assignment

March 6

I MAKE A DIFFERENCE

You are not your career or your resume. Your value doesn't come from anything you own or what neighborhood you live in. All of your value comes from what you have inside—the Divine Seed placed there by your Creator.

If you want to make a difference in the world, you must *let out* the authentic and real you. Only the dreamers make a difference in our world, the men and women who dared to believe in a higher possibility.

What do you ache for? What dream lies dormant within you? What do you need to do to become more authentic?

INSPIRATION
FOR TODAY
*It doesn't interest me
what you do for a living.
I want to know what you
ache for, and if you dare to
dream of meeting your
heart's longing.*
Oriah Mountain
Dreamer
The Invitation

HONORING MY GROWTH

You are your worst critic. The truth is, you're doing the very best you can at any given moment. Given the wisdom you possess, you're making the best choices that can be made.

So, give yourself a break. Stop beating yourself up. No one gets through life without making a few bad choices.

We're not bad people. We're good people who sometimes make bad choices.

Say to yourself each day: "I'm doing the best I can today, and that's good enough. Tomorrow, I will do even better."

NOTES

INSPIRATION
FOR TODAY
*You have not danced so badly, my dear,
Trying to hold hands with the Beautiful One.*

*You have waltzed with great style,
My sweet, crushed angel,
To have ever neared God's Heart at all.*

*Our Partner is notoriously difficult to follow,
And even His best musicians are not always easy
To hear…*
Hafiz
My Sweet, Crushed Angel

March 8

ANSWERING THE CALL

NOTES

At some point we all have to decide on whose authority we stand. Will we let out what we have inside proudly and honorably? Or will we keep hiding who we are, fearing that we're not good enough? To be, or not to be, that is the question. And it is a question we each have to answer for ourselves every day.

INSPIRATION
FOR TODAY
At some stage in life, all thinking beings have to meet the crisis of authority.
Richard Geldard

What God has placed inside you is far too compelling. Eventually you will have to let it loose on the world. It's really just a matter of time. The question isn't whether you will answer your call or not. The question is when!

Spirit is calling—are you listening?

HEAVEN ON EARTH

Your destiny is to manifest the glory of God—to bring heaven to earth. You are here in this life to know what it feels like to be completely loved and accepted, to experience abundance, to be joyous, and to leave behind an example of a life well-lived.

All of the challenges you face are part of your soul's story. They are specific to the lessons you must learn so that you may release fear and finally come to know faith.

Within you has been placed a jewel. It is the Presence of the Divine that is awakening to its destiny. Wake up and realize you already have everything you need to live well and be happy.

NOTES

INSPIRATION FOR TODAY

We are like flies crawling across the ceiling of the Sistine Chapel. We cannot see what angels and gods lie just beneath the threshold of our perceptions.
William Irwin Thompson

SEEING THE GIFT

A gift is something wonderful, something to look forward to receiving. A gift is something that is opened with delight and in anticipation of happiness. There is another meaning for the word "gift." It also means "a talent." Sometimes when we encounter darkness on the path of life, we come away from the experience with a talent we didn't have before. Looking forward to challenging moments in life is not something everyone can do easily. Calling the hard lessons learned "gifts" is not something that everyone can easily do. Perhaps a softer place to start is to ask yourself what talents you've gained as a result of moving through difficult times.

INSPIRATION
FOR TODAY
The wheel of change moves on, and those who were down go up and those who were up go down.
Jawaharlal Nehru

What is going on in your life right now that is challenging? Taking a moment to write down some of the details is one way to begin moving through it.

I AM MADE STRONGER

Consider this: the events of life that are challenging and difficult tend to make us stronger. What, if anything, is your experience of this? How have you come back from hopelessness, distress, sadness or discouragement? What were the turning points and what have you gained through the journey?

NOTES

INSPIRATION
FOR TODAY
*We did not change as we
grew older; we just became
more clearly ourselves.*
Lynn Hall

March 12
I AM WISER

NOTES

Take time to reflect on what you know about life. What have you learned through experience?

Right now, what is happening in your inner world? What wisdom are you acquiring and how are you changing?

INSPIRATION
FOR TODAY
*We would rather be ruined
than changed;/We would
rather die in our dread/
Than climb the cross of the
moment/And let our
illusions die.*
W.H. Auden

GETTING UP AGAIN

What do you do after a fall or disappointment? Get up again. What if you're not inclined to get up again? What if the disappointment is so strong that it leaves you with feelings of sadness or fear?

Don't force yourself to get up again. Eventually the spirit of Life in you will get you up at the appointed time. It might be that for you, the time after the fall is a time to be still and nurture yourself. Time alone in nature is a wonderful healer. Doing something kind for yourself is a wonderful choice. And then, slowly, life in you gets up all by itself.

Can you recall a time when you got up after a fall?

NOTES

INSPIRATION
FOR TODAY

Neither a wise man nor a brave man lies down on the tracks of history to wait for the train of the future to run over him.
Dwight D. Eisenhower

March 14

FINDING THE LIGHT
IN THE DARK

How do you treat yourself after a failure? What is the conversation that goes on in your mind when you have done something that disappoints you? Some people say things to themselves in their own minds that they would never say to another person.

If this is true for you, consider using today as an opportunity to notice when your inner dialogue is disparaging. Simply noticing these moments can have the effect of turning on the lights in a dark room. Just the simple act of stopping. Try it.

INSPIRATION
FOR TODAY
A word of encouragement during a failure is worth more than an hour of praise after success.
Unknown

BEING STILL

In times when your mind is troubled or your experiences are challenging, your thinking can become busy and resistant to one of the most helpful practices that restores us: being still. Perhaps the mind is concerned that being still means forcibly stopping all thinking. Here is a useful approach. First, try being quiet on the outside. Letting your body be motionless is the first stage in being still.

If possible, sit comfortably or lie down and see what happens if you let yourself be as motionless as possible for 10 or 15 minutes. This is a practice that is most beneficial in moments of turmoil.

NOTES

INSPIRATION
FOR TODAY
I have discovered that all human evil comes from this, man's being unable to sit still in the room.
Blaise Pascal

March 16
DARK NIGHT OF THE SOUL

Most people have at least one dark night of the soul. It's a moment of feeling lost, challenged, disoriented, disappointed, disconnected, etc. Why do we go through these times? How do we get through them? What is the value of a dark night of the soul?

What have you learned from going through the dark night of the soul? What new insights did you gain?

INSPIRATION
FOR TODAY
The dark night of the soul—between no longer and not yet.
Joan Borysenko

COMING OUT OF THE DARK

Spiritual growth is all about facing your challenges and moving through them faithfully, instead of being paralyzed by fear. Every great spiritual master has been through periods of darkness and hopelessness. The difference between them and the general population is that they refused to believe the darkness was real. They insisted that only the light was real.

There is no shame in experiencing challenges or going through periods of confusion and uncertainty. But remember: you are not supposed to stay there. You're supposed to return to the light.

There is value to be gained in every step of the spiritual journey. Whether you're basking in the light or hiding in the dark, both conditions bring new awareness.

Do you know someone who is going through a dark period right now? What can you do to support them?

NOTES

INSPIRATION FOR TODAY

Everyone who is destined to have a spiritual transformation comes to the journey with a wound as big as God. There are very few people who become advanced mystics because they simply feel happy on Sunday afternoons.

Andrew Harvey

March 18

MY BURDEN
IS MADE LIGHTER

Take time each day to lighten your load. Be mindful of how much activity is in your life. Slow down. Don't over-commit yourself. Be mindful of the pace at which you are living.

One of the classic symptoms of low self-value is to over schedule and not leave time in your day for self-love and care. Be sure to take care of yourself first, so you can be a source of value in other people's lives.

INSPIRATION
FOR TODAY
*"Calgon,
take me away..."*
Advertisement

How long has it been since you've had a break? When is the last time you took a vacation?

What responsibility or commitment do you need to let go of so you can live a more peaceful life? It's okay to say no. You don't have to do everything yourself.

NO VIRTUE IN SUFFERING

Give up the idea that God is pleased by your suffering. The Infinite is not impressed by how much you endure. It is not withholding its approval or love, waiting to see how strong you are.

No one is "up there" giving brownie points to those who suffer the most. There is no virtue in suffering. No one is ever made better by it. Suffering makes people angry and bitter. It has nothing to do with God's plan for your life.

Whatever you identify yourself with you become like. If you believe in martyrdom, you will live a life of suffering. But if you believe life is about love, joy, ease and abundance—your life will become a joyful experience. The choice is always yours.

INSPIRATION
FOR TODAY
If there is any doubt in your mind as to whether or not God wishes you to have the best, ask yourself: Could God, who is freedom, conceive restriction? Could God, who is limitless, conceive lack...? Could God, who is perfect life, conceive anything that limits the joy of living?
Ernest Holmes
This Thing Called You

I HAVE NO FEAR

NOTES

Fear is what we experience when we step out of our comfort zone, into unknown territory. Since we have no experience "out there," we become afraid at first. Once we gain experience, our fear subsides and we wonder why we were ever afraid.

God lives in the great unknown. That is where your dreams come true, "out there," in the untried. It's where the love of your life waits for you to gain courage to enter.

Step out. Have faith. Follow the call and see where it leads. Great and wise people have always done so.

You are alive only to the degree that you're trying something new. You are dying a little bit each day with each repetition of the things you've always done. Don't die of boredom. Try something new.

What have you been too afraid to try? How much longer will you wait?

BEYOND APPEARANCES

The value of an individual cannot be assessed by looking at the exterior of a body, or by what clothes they wear, or the kind of car they drive. The true value of who we are is contained within. It is the unique, individual soul that lives in the body that has real value. Our genius can't be seen on the outside. Our ability to feel love and compassion isn't visible to others.

Our worth is measured by our capacity to love. Our value is determined by the content of our character, not the size, shape or age of our bodies.

Resist judging others by what society says is important. Give others a chance to reveal their consciousness. Their actions will broadcast who they are.

What judgment do you have of your own appearance? Practice seeing yourself as a spiritual being, not just a body. Look deeply into your eyes in the mirror and practice seeing beyond the reflected image.

NOTES

INSPIRATION
FOR TODAY
Do not judge by appearances, but judge with right judgment.
John 7:24
New American Standard Bible

March 22

I AM FORGIVEN

God lives in the eternal *now*. It has no memory, so it holds no grudge. It has no sequence, so it knows no past. It is Perfect Life, and it knows no error.

You are made in the image and likeness of God. Your true self, the Higher Self remains untouched and unscathed by your earthly experience.

INSPIRATION
FOR TODAY
The practice of forgiveness is our most important contribution to the healing of the world.
Marianne Williamson
A Return to Love

Though your human self has been hurt or wounded, the greater part of you is well and whole. This is not only true for you, but for everyone else as well. With the wisdom we have at the moment, we're all doing the best we can.

Resentment will ruin you. It will take your joy, infect your body and devour your good relationships. You deserve better. Let go of it. Pray to see yourself as God sees you. Pray to see others as God incarnate.

Release your pain. Set your spirit free to join the living again. Return to joy!

THE CIRCLE OF LIFE

One of the oldest symbols for God is the circle—that which has no beginning and no end.

The circle also reminds us that what we send out, must return. It is a spiritual law.

Everything in the universe is in motion. The earth spins on its axis and circles the sun. The galaxy churns round and round. The universe is infinitely expanding.

People are born and die on our planet every day. The only thing that remains constant is our Creator's insatiable desire to make all things new. It has no attachment to form, only to movement and Love's expression. But what God creates is eternal and is never lost.

How do you experience change? Do you try to resist it, or are you willing to go with the flow?

NOTES

INSPIRATION
FOR TODAY
*It's the Circle of Life
And it moves us all
Through despair and hope
Through faith and love
Till we find our place
On the path unwinding
In the Circle*
Tim Rice
The Circle of Life.

March 24

COMPLYING WITH THE LAW

There are certain ways in which creation works that are not negotiable, and these ways are called "laws." Laws are discovered, not invented. They describe what is already in place.

For example, we have to breathe. It isn't negotiable. The consequences of refusing to comply with this law of breathing are catastrophic—if you could actually refuse to breathe, that is. Similarly, objects are drawn towards the center of the planet. It isn't negotiable. Everybody comes back down after they jump up.

INSPIRATION
FOR TODAY
I do not believe that God has imposed suffering upon anyone to punish them or to teach them a lesson.
Ernest Holmes

From your own observation of how life works, what would you say are some of the laws of life? In your response, keep in mind that a law has to apply to all people equally.

NON RESISTANT LIVING

If I know that I have to breath, and I know that I have to come back down after I jump up, and I know that I have to comply with all of the laws of creation, it becomes pointless trying to float or trying not to breathe or trying to do anything that is contrary to the laws of life. The mental, physical and emotional strain of resisting the way things are is exhausting. Once you have discovered the law of fire and understand that it will burn you just like it burns anything else, why put your hand in the fire? If you do put your hand in the fire, why get angry at the fire?

Non-resistant Living means agreeing with life and working with its laws.

Sometimes stress can be an indicator that you are resisting a law of life, or resisting the way things are. Are you resisting anything at the moment?

NOTES

INSPIRATION
FOR TODAY
Nonresistance to evil does not mean absence of any resistance whatsoever but it means not resisting evil with evil but with good.
Mahatma Gandhi

I GIVE MYSELF OVER

NOTES

Giving yourself over is not the same as giving up. It's more like agreeing to let things be since there is no way to change reality. "I give myself over" can be a phrase that is used as an affirmation to remind yourself to relax and yield to the direction of life. The affirmation can be expanded to say "I give myself over to the care and keeping of a universe that works for me."

INSPIRATION
FOR TODAY

When you are nonresistant toward the vision of what you want, your vision runs to meet you. You seldom win until you become willing to do without the prize.
William Frank Diedrich

I LET GO AND SURRENDER

Sometimes people with a tight grip on life are concerned that if they let go, chaos will follow. A leaf floating down a rapidly moving stream stays pretty much safe and intact, almost as if it is skillfully navigating around dangerous rocks and snags. If that leaf somehow had the ability to cling to a rock, the same fast-moving water that was carrying it safely among obstacles would surely apply a dangerous force to the delicate leaf. For the leaf, letting go may be the better option.

Human beings can sometimes find tremendous peace when they first surrender the idea that holding onto a particular thing will bring them safety. For some it is a relationship. For others, it could be a child, or money, or possessions.

Is there something or someone you are holding onto right now? If so, ask yourself what good might come about if you surrender the idea of holding on.

NOTES

INSPIRATION
FOR TODAY
Say to whatever seems worth having: If you do not want me as much as I want you, I do not want you at all. I can do without you and sorrow not; but I will welcome you if you come. Take your choice. It does not matter to me.
Imelda Shanklin

March 28

FOLLOWING THE WAY

NOTES

Life is going to take you where it is going. Freedom in this matter is paradoxical: we have no choice when it comes to being alive, but we certainly have choice as to our internal response to life. Another way of saying the same thing is I can decide to enjoy the ride, or not, but I will continue to be on the ride one way or another.

INSPIRATION
FOR TODAY
*Non-resistance
is not indifference to,
but rather confidence in,
the will of God.*
Source Unknown

Which way is your life going? Is it the way of the free-flowing stream fulfilling its journey, or is it the way of resistance and clinging, or something else altogether?

Look for the way in your life; the area where things flow. And follow it.

GRACE

Grace is the gift of Spirit that comes without conditions. In a way of speaking, it is everything life placed in you—and it is still there now—awaiting recognition. When people say "by the grace of God..." I believe they are talking about those times when all other skills, talents and knowledge give way and what is left is undefended love and acceptance for ourselves and the world.

What does grace mean to you?

NOTES

_____

_____

_____

_____

_____

INSPIRATION
FOR TODAY

Grace isn't a little prayer you chant before receiving a meal. It's a way to live.
Jackie Windspear

_____

_____

_____

_____

_____

_____

_____

_____

_____

March 30
SAY YES

Try this for your focus today: repeat to yourself frequently, "I live in a universe that works for me and not to me." Say it to yourself often as you move through the day. Then, as the day progresses, notice anything that seems to be happening to you and pause for a moment to ask yourself "What if this is exactly the way the universe is trying to support me?"

INSPIRATION
FOR TODAY
The way to develop self-confidence is to do the thing you fear and get a record of successful experiences behind you.
William Jennings Byron

Sit with the question and listen for your own wisdom. This is a way of saying yes to life.

INTERDEPENDENT

When the Declaration of Independence was written, nations were separated by great distances and travel was difficult. But 21st century technology has erased those distances. We are becoming a truly interdependent society, whether we like it or not.

Our future is tied to what we do together, not as nations acting against each other and for themselves alone. We have evolved to reach our destiny where we must now take care of *all* of our people, not just the favored few.

All families have to make decisions and choices that are best for the whole family, not just one member. We are becoming *one* human family on earth whose future will be determined by all of us together.

How is this new paradigm of interdependence showing up in your life?

NOTES

INSPIRATION FOR TODAY

...what worked before will now destroy us. We must rapidly stop doing what we have done so successfully—building, overpopulating, polluting, and using up nonrenewable resources to survive.
Barbara Marx Hubbard
Conscious Evolution

April 1
SHARED VALUES

Lots of people say how much they value their loved ones or their spiritual growth. But talk is cheap. What do you spend your money on? That's what you value the most.

In order to be in a relationship with someone, it's not important that you have the same interests, religion or race. But you must have the same values. If your number one value is honesty and theirs is money, it's impossible to be together.

INSPIRATION
FOR TODAY
You can find out what you value the most by looking at your bank statement.
Chris Michaels

You can find out what you value the most by asking yourself, "What is most important to me in life?"

Make a list of your top five values and then compare them to the values of your spouse, friends or family. Such a list may include honesty, spiritual growth, love, or a personal relationship with God.

After you make your list, open your checkbook and see if you are putting your money where your values are.

EMBRACING ONENESS

There are many different religions and cultural beliefs practiced in our world, each with has its own customs and personality. However, we all share one thing in common: we are spiritual beings living through human bodies. We are connected on a soul-to-soul level with everything that is alive.

When we sense our oneness with each other, we honor the sacred presence of the *one* Life in us all. We feel bonded to each other in friendship and love.

Trouble only arises when we feel separate and apart from the Source of our good, when we feel disconnected from our fellow human beings.

Regardless of how we feel, the truth does not change. We are all *one*! Sometimes we are able to recognize that truth—and other times, we forget.

What do you do to remember our oneness? What happens when you feel connected to God? What happens when you don't?

NOTES

INSPIRATION
FOR TODAY
God is the I of the infinite.
Hugo

April 3

EMBRACING
OUR DIFFERENCES

It's difficult to imagine the creative genius of the Artist who designed every snowflake to be different, and every person's DNA to be unique. We cannot fathom our Creator's infinite Mind. But we can appreciate its creation.

No one is like you. No one thinks or feels exactly the way you do. You are a unique creation, a once-in-a-lifetime opportunity for God to express. Your happiness does not come from trying to get others to be more like you, or from pretending to be like someone else. It comes from having the courage to be yourself and from embracing others who are different.

INSPIRATION
FOR TODAY
I do not wonder at a snowflake, a shell, a summer landscape, or the glory of the stars; but at the necessity of beauty under which the universe lies.
Ralph Waldo Emerson

Who do you know who is completely different from you? What do you admire about them? What do you respect? What value do you see in the differences between you?

CARING

In order to be healthy and stay happy, your soul needs to care for someone or some thing. It also needs to feel cared for by others. Love and care are to the soul what food is to your body. It is a basic necessity for living.

This doesn't mean you have to be married or in an intimate relationship with someone to fulfill your soul's desire. It means there must be someone or something you care deeply about. It could be a pet, friend, your family or church. It could be a cause you feel passionate about.

INSPIRATION FOR TODAY
One of the oldest human needs is having someone to wonder where you are when you don't come home at night.
Margaret Mead

What do you care the most about? Who do you care for? Who cares for you?

Too often, our true feelings go unspoken. Think of ways you can activate your caring. Make a care list and then do something special for the people on your list.

NOTES

April 5
SYNCHRONICITY

There are no coincidences in life, only events we can't explain.

When you have eyes to see, the wisdom you seek will find you. When you have ears to hear, you will hear exactly what you've been waiting so long to hear. When the student is ready, the teacher appears.

INSPIRATION
FOR TODAY
*When you're on
the right path, Spirit
will wink at you.*
Chris Michaels
Your Soul's Assignment

Spirit is at work in your life arranging things and making plans for your greater good. It is placing on your path exactly what you need in order to succeed and be happy. Wake up. Look around. There's something or someone near you trying to get your attention.

If the choices you are making are in alignment with Spirit, It will give you a wink just to let you know you're going in the right direction. When that happens, give God a wink back just to say, "Thanks, God. I got it."

ONE HUMAN FAMILY

There is only *one* race of people on our planet. It is the human race. We are all part of one human family. The sooner we realize this, the sooner we will stop killing each other in wars. When we realize that the children dying in Africa are *our* children, we will make it a priority to feed them.

We have each been created as a unique individual, but we come from *one* Creator. That means we're all brothers and sisters—connected by our souls.

The challenge is for us to stop dreaming that we're separate, and wake up to the reality that we are all *one.*

NOTES

INSPIRATION
FOR TODAY
*If I can stop one
heart from breaking,
I shall not live in vain:
If I can ease one
life the aching,
Or cool one pain,
Or help one fainting robin
Unto his nest again,
I shall not live in vain.*
Emily Dickinson

April 7
GETTING INTO LISTENING

I saw a cartoon strip in which a little girl looks up at her father, who is reading the newspaper, and says, "Dad, you have to listen to me with your eyes as well as your ears." Listening, for me, is something that requires a conscious choice to go beyond the surface experience of hearing words. It means to listen to the message of what is being said between and beyond the words.

INSPIRATION FOR TODAY

I know that you believe you understand what you think I said, but I'm not sure you realize that what you heard is not what I meant.
Robert McCloskey

I think that people who have trained themselves to truly hear what others are saying are in possession of tremendous personal strength and become helpful, even influential among friends and colleagues.

I think that people who have trained themselves to listen to what Life is saying are in possession of tremendous personal power and become more trusting of their intuition because they have learned to go beyond the surface, and catch the vision of what is the highest good for all concerned.

MAINTAINING SELF-IDENTITY

Listening deeply and carefully to others builds rapport and understanding and activates compassion. It can also help the one listening to become very clear about their own preferences and identity.

Today, as you listen to others, let your purpose be to remain aware of both your similarities to and differences from the speaker.

NOTES

INSPIRATION
FOR TODAY
*The value of identity of
course is that so often with
it comes purpose.*
Richard R. Grant

April 9

I DON'T HAVE TO FIX OTHERS

The best quick fix I ever had was a visit to my grandmother for a good venting. She would always listen attentively, nod frequently in understanding, and express appropriate agreement with my outrage. Regardless of the severity of the case, the impossibility of the problem, or the chaos in my mind, her one simple response was almost always, "It will all work out in the end...it always does."

INSPIRATION
FOR TODAY
*The first duty of love—
is to listen.*
Paul Tillich

There were times when her response would be frustrating. However, in retrospect, I see how much more I preferred her "non-fixing" response to my problems over the advice of many well-meaning friends who sometimes asked, "Have you tried this?" or "have you tried that?"

Do you try to fix other people when they talk to you about their difficulties? How might it be for you if today you offer no advice or opinion on anything? Try it for one day. Just listen.

April 10

AFFECTION

People experience and express affection in different ways. What makes you feel cared for? Is it the quality time someone spends with you? Or is it in a warm hug from a friend? For some, caring comes through a thoughtful card or when someone does a thoughtful service for them, like taking out the garbage. Still others need to hear caring expressed in words, while others feel it best when their privacy is respected. Curiously, the way one person experiences affection is not necessarily the same for others. Even close family members, partners and loved ones can have dissimilar modes of caring. You may love a hug whereas it may do very little for your sibling.

Learning to recognize the way others express caring is a way of developing sensitivity and understanding, both of which are essential if you want to activate compassion in your life. Who are the important people in your life, and what are their various ways of expressing affection?

NOTES

INSPIRATION
FOR TODAY
*Self interest is the enemy
of all true affection.*
Franklin D. Roosevelt

Spirit Is Calling • 101

April 11

LET IT BE

_____

_____

_____

_____

_____

_____

_____

_____

_____

_____

_____

_____

INSPIRATION
FOR TODAY
*Only by acceptance of the
past, can you alter it.*
T. S. Eliot

The average person's mind dashes from one opinion to the other, often lingering on the past and the future. If you took a moment to sit in a public place such as a shopping mall, watching the activities around you, you might notice that it is a bit like eavesdropping on your very own mind. You'd probably hear bits of conversations that reflect the whole range of human states of mind. Wanting, preferring, hating, loving, worrying, controlling, etc. If you were actually sitting in the mall, you wouldn't do anything about the bits of conversation you pick up. You would just notice them.

If you could do the same thing with your mind, you would be practicing a type of meditation, noticing what passes through, assigning each thought to a category, but not doing much about what you witness other than experiencing it.

In the next few moments, what categories of thought pass through your mind?

THIS TOO SHALL PASS

Learning how to talk to and be with a person who is in crisis or upset is a beautiful skill. Anyone who is willing to let things be and to stay present with a troubled person can develop this skill. Possibly the most important thing to do for a loved one in crisis is to love them.

NOTES

*INSPIRATION
FOR TODAY
In helping others,
we shall help ourselves,
for whatever good we give
out completes the circle
and comes back to us.*
Flora Edwards

April 13

EMPATHY VERSUS SYMPATHY

Understanding requires us to really listen with an attitude of openness. In this way, your listening can draw you close to the experience of the speaker as you get closer to their world through their telling. There is a line of closeness that is not advisable to cross. That is the line beyond which you begin to experience the speaker's experience as your own, rather than feeling honored to witness someone else's story.

INSPIRATION
FOR TODAY
The great gift of human beings is that we have the power of empathy.
Meryl Streep

RESOLVING INNER CONFLICT

Y ou were created as an individual to travel your own route to Truth. You must resolve the conflict in your mind between the Truth and the lies you have accepted as true. Every person has to do this for themselves. Resolution comes from separating opinions and judgments from the Universal Truth (that which is true for all people, all of the time).

It is written that Jesus said, "You shall know the truth and the truth shall set you free." But, knowing the truth rarely comes in a flash, all at once. It is usually achieved over time through self-evaluation. We have to find our own answers to questions like these: Is there a God? Is God a Power for Good? Does God want good for my life? Am I worthy of receiving that good?

Take time today to address the bigger issues of life. Ask yourself the questions listed above. Begin weeding out the lies, judgments and opinions of others. It's okay to question.

NOTES

INSPIRATION
FOR TODAY
*To believe with certainty
we must begin by doubting.*
Stanislaus

April 15

I AM GREATER
THAN MY PAST

NOTES

NOTES

_____

_____

_____

_____

_____

_____

_____

_____

_____

_____

_____

_____

_____

Lots of people die of boredom. Sometimes it takes the body a while to manifest the disease the doctor says finally did them in, but they really died of boredom. They got tired of repeating the same negative pattern year after year, after year. So the body responded by setting the spirit free of the circular pattern they were stuck repeating.

INSPIRATION
FOR TODAY
*The definition of insanity
is doing the same thing
over and over again,
expecting different results.*
Rita Mae Brown

The truth is that every day is a brand new chance to start over. It is filled with new opportunities to think differently and be different. You don't have to repeat the past. You can overcome it. You don't have to be limited by your past. You can start a new chapter in your life, right now! It's as easy as making a choice to do so, and sticking with it.

What event, experience or idea in your past would you like to heal? What do you need to say in order to move on? What do you need to do, so you can finally leave it in the past where it belongs?

I AM NOT MY CURRENT CONDITION

All conditions are temporary. They are a picture of the effects of your thinking. Just as a photograph captures who you were at the moment the camera lens opened and recorded your image, conditions represent who you were at that precise moment in time. Your current conditions represent your past thinking and beliefs. They change every time you have a new thought.

You are the creator of the conditions in your life; the ones you're proud of and the ones you wish would go away. That puts you in the seat of power, with authority over your life. When you change your thinking, the condition will change.

What condition do you want to change/heal/overcome? What new idea do you need to incorporate into your thinking that will change it?

NOTES

INSPIRATION FOR TODAY

When we bring a lamp into a darkened room, where does the darkness go? It never was a thing of itself, merely a condition. And we have power over conditions.
Ernest Holmes

April 17

I DETERMINE MY FUTURE

You are not a victim of circumstances or mysterious events. You are the co-creator of your life. You partner with Spirit every time you think. Your thought creates your world of experience. Your power lies in what you are thinking at any given moment and the power to change your life is just one thought away.

INSPIRATION
FOR TODAY
You are the one! You are the one you need to depend on. You are the one you need to make demands on. You are the one you need to love, to honor, to respect, to rely upon, and to listen to before all others.
Dr. Kennedy Shultz
You are the Power

You do not have to repeat the past. You do not have to be a victim ever again. You can create a bright, new future.

Take a stand for who you are. Shout out to the universe: "I am not a victim. I am a partner with God, creating a wonderful life."

I AM THE AUTHOR
OF MY STORY

Because you have been endowed by your Creator with free will, you have the choice to think however and whatever you like. *But*—what you choose to give your thought to must produce an effect. All thought is creative. Therefore, you are the author of your life's experience every time you think.

You are the author and God is the producer. It takes your script and brings it to life by attracting to you all of the characters and events in the drama.

You have the choice to re-write your script anytime you like. What re-writes would you like to make today?

NOTES

INSPIRATION
FOR TODAY
We need to teach the next generation of children from Day One that they are responsible for their lives. Mankind's greatest gift, also its greatest curse, is that we have free choice. We can make our choices built from love or from fear.
Elisabeth Kubler-Ross

April 19
CREATING A NEW STORY

I have a friend who repeats herself often. She tells the same story over and over again, forgetting she's told it before. When this happens, I listen patiently until she's finished and then remind her I've heard that one before.

Being actively engaged in life means creating *new* stories. It means making a conscious effort to meet new people, go to new places and try different things.

INSPIRATION
FOR TODAY
The self is not something that one finds. It is something that one creates.
Thomas Szasz

It's easy to get stuck in a rut, repeating the same experience over and over again. We enjoy the comfort of our favorite people and foods. Creating something new requires a period of uncertainty and uncomfortableness and that's something most people try to avoid.

Live consciously. Choose to do something new today. Make yourself uncomfortable...or else you may end up like my friend, just repeating the same old story over and over again.

TRUTH VERSUS FICTION

Truth is like the light in a room; once it's turned on, there is no room for the darkness of lies. They immediately return to the nothingness from which they came. That which is True about you is eternal. Everything else is temporary.

You are more than the facts of your life or the opinions of others. You are more than your history of accomplishments or the assets you have accumulated. You are the Truth in action—the Presence of God displaying itself in the world.

The spiritual journey is about separating the Truth about you from the fiction you've been told. This reinstatement of Truth has to be accomplished in your mind. It begins with the first question to ask on your journey: who am I?

Don't rush to find an answer! This is not a race. Just "be" in the question for a while, letting the wisdom rise up from within in its own time and sequence.

NOTES

INSPIRATION
FOR TODAY
*Truth exists.
Only lies are invented.*
Georges Braque

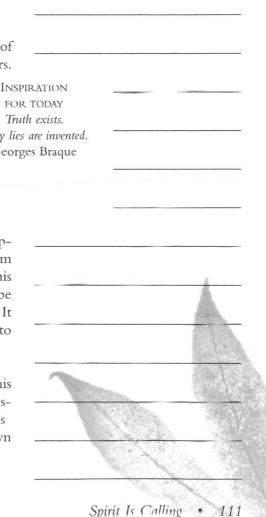

COMPASSIONATE CARE

NOTES

The word "compassion" is made up of two parts. The first means "with" or "together," and the second means "with strong feeling." In other words, compassion describes the ability to identify and understand the experience of someone else who might be in distress. It is important, then, for a person to understand themselves if they are ever to be compassionate.

The strong feelings of compassion come from a sense of shared experience and are frequently combined with a desire to relieve the suffering of another.

What do you have compassion for?

ONLY LOVE LASTS

I remember stopping at an estate sale for a person who had died without family descendants. Being of advanced age, all of her friends had predeceased her too. As I looked through the items of her estate, I came upon a box of cards and photos in which were messages of appreciation and love from long past friends and family. I didn't know this woman, but in a short while I felt the love she had left behind and I purchased the box of memories to keep among my most treasured items. Whenever I see it, I wonder what love I am contributing in the world and the impact it may have on people I will never know.

NOTES

INSPIRATION FOR TODAY

The only measure of your words and your deeds, Will be the love you leave behind when you're done.
Fred Small

April 23

THE WAY OF THE SPIRIT

Spiritual seekers have searched for the meaning of life and for ultimate truth by asking such questions as these: Why am I here? What is the meaning of life? What is mine to do?

Why are you here?

INSPIRATION
FOR TODAY
When you discover your mission, you will feel its demand. It will fill you with enthusiasm and a burning desire to get to work on it.
W. Clement Stone

GLORIOUS WORK

The fifth of the eight elements of the Buddhist Noble Eightfold Path is "Right Livelihood." It has to do with the way we choose to earn our living and the ethical implications of the work we do. Broadly speaking, right livelihood has a beneficial impact on the world while wrong livelihood is to the detriment of both the world and the one doing the work.

When instructing his followers, Buddha made suggestions about how to follow right livelihood. He advised his followers to avoid work that requires deceit, hypocrisy, trickery or any kind of dishonest way of acquiring business or customers.

At the heart of right livelihood is compassion and love for others. Activating compassion in your life can help you determine what is the right way for you to work in the world.

NOTES

INSPIRATION
FOR TODAY
Being happy at work makes you more energetic, productive, motivated, creative and successful. That is what we need more of. That is how we will work from now on. With happiness.
Alexander Kjerulf

April 25

SEEING SPIRIT EVERYWHERE

How can we see God, who is invisible and infinite in things and people? Jesus asked his followers a similar question when he asked them how it was possible to believe a person who said they loved God, who cannot be seen, when they were not able to love their neighbors, whom they can see.

INSPIRATION
FOR TODAY
*You have it in your power
to make your days on
Earth a path of flowers,
instead of a path of thorns.*
Sri Sathya Sai Baba

Today try this experiment. Whenever you remember to do so, pause and look around you and make a mental list of everything you see. As you name each item, say silently to yourself "Somehow, this is Spirit in form."

SHARING EVERYTHING

Norman Macewan said that happiness is not so much in having as sharing and that we make a living by what we get, but we make a life by what we give. Use today to make a mental inventory of what you have in your life that you could share. This list could include the tangible as well as items such as friendship, leisure time, etc.

Choose something from your list and share it by giving a portion of it away to someone. You could choose someone within your circle of family and friends, or to be really adventurous, choose someone you do not know that well.

NOTES

INSPIRATION
FOR TODAY

Those who bring sunshine into the lives of others, cannot keep it from themselves.
James M. Barrie

April 27

A MODEL OF COMPASSION

NOTES

INSPIRATION
FOR TODAY
A generous heart, kind speech, and a life of service and compassion are the things which renew humanity.
Buddha

Florence Nightingale, the lady of the lamp, was raised in affluence. Throughout her gentle, shy childhood, she was fascinated with the process of restoring living creatures back to health. She dreamed of becoming a nurse. Legend has it that her father attempted to discourage her by saying, "You will not be able to change all of the sadness and poverty in the world." To which Florence replied, "I will make the world a better place." She went to nursing school, and when England and France went to war with Russia, she led a contingent of nurses to staff a shabby, dirty, rat-infested hospital on the front lines. None of the women were prepared for what they saw, so they simply set out to provide compassionate care, cleaning, cooking, feeding, and helping. Out of their work a deep respect, love and dedication grew for the nurses, in particular for Florence who was seemingly everywhere at once. At night, her lamp burned as she walked the four miles of corridors among the rows of damaged soldiers who were comforted just by seeing her pass by.

I AM CONNECTED TO OTHERS

It doesn't take a rocket scientist to figure out that we each live in a separate body. But if you look below the surface level, you will see that our bodies all contain the same material or energy, even though each is assembled in a unique pattern.

This same truth applies to our spirit or soul. We are all connected to each other on multiple levels. That's why we feel compassion for others when they experience pain or loss, and joy when they fulfill their dreams.

You are not alone. You never have been. You are part of an intricate web of life. Reach out and touch others. Extend yourself emotionally and feel your connection to the Whole. Let yourself be vulnerable. There is great power that comes from being open, even if you get hurt occasionally.

NOTES

INSPIRATION
FOR TODAY
*A human being
is a part of a whole,
called by us "universe"...*
Albert Einstein

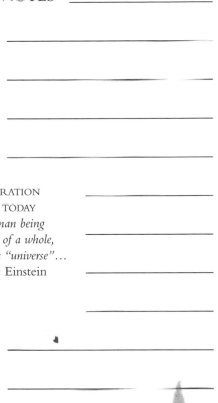

April 29
SOUL TO SOUL

We are not meant to live our lives alone. We need to connect with other people on a "soul-to-soul" level. This can be done through intimate partnerships, close friendships, involvement in a spiritual community, or many other ways. We sense our *oneness* through our connection to others. By relating to them, we find our common heritage and ancestry. We bond with a common purpose.

INSPIRATION
FOR TODAY
We are drawn together by nature—because what we can be together far exceeds what any of us can apart.
Chris Michaels
Your Soul's Assignment

Who do you connect with on a soul-to-soul level? What do you value most about your relationship? What have you learned about yourself by your association with them?

THE ONE BECOMES THE MANY

The spokes of a wheel all converge in the middle to form a single point. At that point, there is no motion, friction or energy spent. And yet without it, there could be no wheel. This is a metaphor for Spirit. It is the *one* that creates and propels the many.

You are one spoke in the wheel of life, permanently connected to the Center, the Source, God! Your life comes from that Source. It is propelled and animated by it.

Although your connection to Spirit can never be severed, sometimes you feel it and sometimes you don't. When you feel connected to Spirit, you are happier and healthier in mind and body. When you don't, you make poor choices.

What spiritual practice can you engage in that will help you feel more closely connected to Spirit?

NOTES

INSPIRATION
FOR TODAY
*We join thirty spokes
to the hub of a wheel,
yet it's the center hole
that drives the chariot.*
The Tao

May 1

YOUR LOVED ONES

Contrary to popular belief, we do not choose whom we love. Love chooses for us and draws them to us. They are near to us because Love has an unannounced plan for our togetherness. Growth is the plan.

Sometimes the people we love the most are the same ones who annoy us the most. They challenge us to be more patient and compassionate. They call on our strength when we feel weak. They ask for forgiveness when we'd much rather hang on to our resentment.

> INSPIRATION
> FOR TODAY
> *There is no remedy for love*
> *but to love more.*
> Thoreau

Our loved ones usually demand more from us than anyone else we know. And that's because they see something in us no one else sees. They see our innate Divine potential. They see our spiritual possibility.

Love isn't blind. On the contrary; it grants perfect clarity. It allows you to see through the human imperfections straight through to the perfect soul inside.

WALKING TOGETHER

You share two things in common with every person on earth: Divine Potential and human pain. The first is the source of your dream for a greater life and better experience. Divine potential is innate. It must be let out and then followed like a vision. That you can do alone.

But the second thing you have in common with others; your human pain was not meant to be borne alone. For that, we need others to give us strength and the assurance that even though appearances say otherwise, in truth all is well.

Who is your best friend? Who do you call when you are in pain?

NOTES

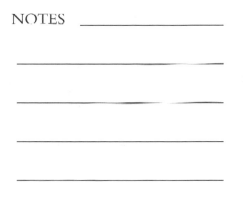

INSPIRATION
FOR TODAY
I keep my friends as misers do their treasure, because, of all things granted us by wisdom, none is greater or better than friendship.
Pietro Aretino

MY NEW LIFE

No relationship is an even balance between give and take. Sometimes our friends or spouses give 70 percent while we give just 30 percent. And sometimes it's reversed. Rarely is it ever a fifty-fifty exchange. Sometimes they need more support than we do, and vice versa.

INSPIRATION
FOR TODAY
*Rain does not fall
on one roof alone.*
Cameroonian proverb

No one is strong and well-balanced emotionally, physically and spiritually *all* of the time. Everybody needs a shoulder to cry on occasionally. Everybody needs someone to carry their burdens once in a while.

Who do you lean on? Who leans on you?

THE POWER OF COMMUNITY

We are stronger together than we are apart. What we can accomplish together far exceeds what anyone can do on their own. People who come together in community around a cause can bring an ocean of change. That's why fearful dictators pass laws against public assembly. They fear being overthrown by the powerful consciousness of a mass of people.

Community builds character and strength. It bonds us to each other and holds us accountable for our morality. It reminds us of our past and brings us hope for a better future. It is a place of sanctuary when we are hurting or in need of support. It is a place of inspiration when we need faith.

What communities are you a part of? What value do they bring to your life? How do you support them?

NOTES _____

INSPIRATION
FOR TODAY
*Strangely enough,
I can never be what I ought
to be until you are what
you ought to be.*
Dr. Martin
Luther King, Jr.

May 5

COMING BACK TOGETHER

NOTES

Community is important to us because it is through community that we can activate our oneness. Community is the way we feel our connection to each other and to the Universe. American philosopher Ernest Holmes said that it's a simple proposition: everyone must love and be loved or he/she will not be fulfilled or happy.

INSPIRATION
FOR TODAY
A community is like a ship; everyone ought to be prepared to take the helm.
Henrik Ibsen

I don't think he was talking about romantic love. I think he was talking about the kind of loving kindness that is to be found in groups of people who care about each other. In today's society it is easy to live a solitary life and minimize the exposure you have to other people. This makes community something that requires conscious choice and endeavor.

Describe your current experience of community.

I AM SAFE

Activating community as a spiritual value in your life can be facilitated by taking an inventory of just how welcoming you are to others, and how comfortable you feel around others. When you read the title of today's journal entry, "I Am Safe," what comes to mind? Take a moment to reflect on the phrase from two distinct angles: How safe am I to be around? How safe do I feel around others? Your responses will provide the foundation for activating a sense of community in your life.

NOTES

INSPIRATION
FOR TODAY
I am of the opinion that my life belongs to the whole community and as long as I live, it is my privilege to do for it whatever I can.
George Bernard Shaw

May 7
I TRUST OTHERS

To activate trust in your life, you have to be able to expose your vulnerabilities to others with confidence that they will not take advantage of your defenselessness. There is a degree of risk involved, because the probability of being hurt can never be assessed 100%. Nevertheless, the condition of being able to be fully helpless in the presence of another is the cornerstone of community.

Poet Dina Maria Mulock Craik said, "Oh, the comfort ...the inexpressible comfort of feeling safe with a person having neither to weigh thought or measure words, but pouring them all right out just as they are, chaff and grain together, certain that a faithful hand will take and sift them, keep what is worth keeping, and with a breath of kindness blow the rest away."

Where in your community do you feel safe?

INSPIRATION
FOR TODAY
While the spirit of neighborliness was important on the frontier because neighbors were so few, it is even more important now because our neighbors are so many.
Lady Bird Johnson

I AM TRUSTWORTHY

What makes you trust-worthy? Can your word be counted on? Would it be reasonable for your friends and neighbors to have a confident expectancy that you will treat them honorably?

To activate trust in your life and become trustworthy involves taking responsibility for your conduct and obligations so that you become a person who warrants trust.

A measure of your trust-worthiness may be found in how safe your friends and neighbors feel around you.

Find ways to complete this sentence: "I am worthy of trust because..."

NOTES

INSPIRATION
FOR TODAY
You may be deceived if you trust too much, but you will live in torment unless you trust enough.
Frank Crane

FAITH IN ACTION

Part of navigating through life depends on our ability to forecast what lies ahead. We create expectations of our community based on our experiences and we use these experiences, to determine what to trust and what not to trust. However, realistically, in community the variables are too great to accurately predict behavior and often we find ourselves in a position where we do not have full knowledge of individuals, their intent or history.

INSPIRATION
FOR TODAY
Faith is putting all your eggs in God's basket, then counting your blessings before they hatch.
Ramona C. Carroll

Activating faith in community is about going ahead and taking the risk to treat people around you as if they can reliably be expected to be kind, truthful and open hearted, to the best of their ability.

What risks of faith are you willing to take today?

I FOLLOW MY HEART

A community is more than the people in it. It is something that reaches beyond the individuals who make it up. However, each individual in the community contributes something unique and indispensable.

What do you bring to your community that you alone can bring?

INSPIRATION
FOR TODAY
Always be a first-rate version of yourself, instead of a second-rate version of somebody else.
Judy Garland

NOTES _____

_____

_____

_____

_____

_____

_____

_____

_____

_____

_____

_____

_____

FEARLESS LIVING

NOTES _____

_____

_____

_____

_____

_____

_____

_____

_____

_____

_____

_____

_____

_____

_____

Activating community in your life demands relationships with people that you will some day have a whole range of experiences with. In community you get to be vulnerable, strong, insecure, creative and everything else, too. With this in mind, doing your best is different from looking your best. One is achievable and the other is unreliable at best.

INSPIRATION
FOR TODAY
Once you've been really "bad" in a movie, there's a certain kind of fearlessness you develop.
Jack Nicholson

Doing your best may be likened to living fearlessly. It has less to do with getting an A on your report card than it has to do with accepting yourself and trusting that exactly who you are is exactly what the community needs.

I AM FRIENDLY

It costs nothing to be kind to others and yet it brings an abundance of good in return.

Too many people are waiting to be friendly. They're like victims waiting for the next disaster. They think kindness is given only when something warrants it. They're only willing to give what they receive first. If someone smiles, they smile back. If someone gives a compliment first, they give one in return.

Ghandi said, "Be the change you want to see in the world." In other words, give the very thing you want to receive in return.

Be friendly to others, even if they aren't kind to you first. Give to them what you want to receive.

NOTES

INSPIRATION
FOR TODAY
The best portion of a good man's life, His little, nameless, unremembered acts, Of kindness and of love.
Wordsworth

LOVE IS KNOCKING

At the end of our lives, the only thing that really matters is how much we loved. Nothing else is important.

The good news is is that even if we have missed every opportunity to love, another one is just around the corner. Love comes knocking over and over again, until we finally have the courage to go to the door. Love is most persistent!

INSPIRATION
FOR TODAY
When love beckons to you,
follow him, though his
ways are hard and steep...
Kahlil Gibran

Love always brings challenge. It was designed that way. Because in the end, Love's goal is to *transform* us from mere mortals into gods. It remakes us from the inside, out.

What opportunities are present in your life today to love? What or who is knocking at your door?

SURROUNDED BY LOVE

Love has its own agenda for your life. It can't be planned, organized or strategized. It will not be manipulated or bargained for. Love will not fit into your plans. It is not supposed to be convenient. In fact, there's nothing more inconvenient than Love.

Love doesn't come *from* other people. It comes *through* them. God is the only true Source of Love.

You are surrounded by and immersed in Love. You don't go in search of what's already there. That would be like a fish swimming in the ocean looking for water.

Feel the Presence of the Love that surrounds you. Let its gentle embrace comfort you. Follow your heart. It will lead to your destiny.

NOTES

INSPIRATION
FOR TODAY
*Love takes us out of life
and away from the plans
we have made for our lives.*
Thomas Moore
Care of the Soul

May 15

OPPORTUNITIES TO CONNECT

NOTES

Every day is a new opportunity to meet someone new. Who knows what joy this new person might bring to your life? Could they be a future friend, lover or partner in business? Do they have the answer to the question you've been asking yourself for years? What good do they have to bring to your life?

INSPIRATION
FOR TODAY
Hold a true friend with both your hands.
Nigerian proverb

Just the opposite is true as well. Every day is a new opportunity for you to bless someone else's life. What good do you have to contribute to them? What wisdom do you have to convey? What value can you bring to their life?

The people who enter your world are not there by accident or coincidence. They are scheduled to come in and out of your life at the precise time they can contribute something of value. Watch closely. Stay alert. Be conscious of every opportunity.

DRAW NEAR
TO EACH OTHER

Nothing brings us closer than a shared adversity. When there is an earthquake or terrorist attack, suddenly we draw near to each other to gather strength and comfort. The Inner Knower is activated and we suddenly remember we're all *one*.

But, you don't have to wait until you face some challenge to get close to someone else. You can do so by making a conscious effort.

Who is present in your life today that you would like to be closer with? What can you do to make that happen?

NOTES

INSPIRATION
FOR TODAY
That which does not kill me makes me stronger.
Nietzsche

May 17

LOVE AND LAUGHTER

Joy and laughter are by-products of love. One comes first and then the other.

If you start by learning to love yourself first, happiness will follow. Don't try to make yourself happy. Start by finding something you can love about yourself first, and happiness will come along as an effect.

What do you love about yourself? Make a list of 10 things you love about yourself. Then, make another list of 10 things that bring you the most joy in life. Compare the lists.

CULTIVATING COMMUNITY

Every five seconds a child dies of hunger in our world. That's about 16,000 children each day. We have enough food to feed them all, but the boundaries between nations and the corruption of leaders prevent us from doing so.

Becoming *one* global community will end this injustice. When we realize that all of the children on earth belong to us, we will see to it that they are fed.

What can you do to help raise the consciousness of our world? What difference can you make in your local community?

INSPIRATION
FOR TODAY
*It takes a village
to raise a child.*
African proverb

NOTES _____

_____

_____

_____

_____

_____

_____

_____

_____

_____

_____

_____

May 19

UNITY NOT UNIFORMITY

Humanity is made up of endless numbers of individuals who are not the same. Together, these unique individuals form a community and share common traits. Appreciating both the similarities and differences between the people who make up a community allows for a common vision to be fulfilled without sacrificing the value of diversity.

INSPIRATION
FOR TODAY
The unity of freedom has never relied on uniformity of opinion.
John Fitzgerald Kennedy

Some people allow differences of opinion, style, and taste to block intimacy and progress. What would be different in your life if differences in opinions, philosophy, and choice were encouraged and welcomed? If this is already the case in your community, how does it influence you?

BEYOND TOLERANCE

Tolerance means the acceptance of different views among people in regards to religion, politics, choices, etc. In a sense, the word "tolerate" suggests the act of putting up with these differences. In this light, tolerance is a good thing to foster in a community. However, for safety and thriving to take place, perhaps there is a step beyond tolerating differences. Perhaps there is a way in which differences can not only be put up with, but celebrated, without losing any sense of individual freedom.

There is another meaning to the word "tolerance" that has to do with the ability to survive and withstand tough conditions. This could be a valuable skill when you find yourself in a community where your opinion is the minority and your differences are tolerated but not celebrated.

When in life have you found yourself to be in the minority and how did you maintain the integrity of your soul?

NOTES

INSPIRATION
FOR TODAY
You have your way.
I have my way. As for
the right way, the correct
way, and the only way,
it does not exist.
Friedrich Nietzsche

May 21

ACCEPTING DIFFERENCES

NOTES

Accepting differences may be easier when you find yourself in the majority and your way of being is the strongest thread in a community. When you are a member of the majority, it is easy to minimize or overlook the opinion or needs of the smallest group within the community. Accepting differences can include noticing that they exist, and paying attention to them, especially if you are in a position to welcome those who are different, or unlike the rest of the group.

INSPIRATION
FOR TODAY
*In the practice of tolerance,
one's enemy is
the best teacher.*
Dalai Lama

What are the minority groups in your community and how do you welcome them?

RESPECTING OTHERS

Activating spirituality in your daily life develops your sense of self as you begin to explore your place in the Universe. With this comes a personal awareness of your uniqueness and with that an appreciation of the uniqueness of the people around you. You may discover, as you continue to activate daily spirituality in your life, that a softening occurs around any need you might have to attain approval. You may discover a willingness to listen without being persuaded and a growing ability to maintain your course while letting others follow theirs.

What changes are you noticing in your life?

NOTES _____

_____

_____

_____

_____

_____

INSPIRATION
FOR TODAY
As we grow as unique persons, we learn to respect the uniqueness of others.
Robert H. Schuller

_____

_____

_____

_____

_____

_____

_____

_____

DIFFERENT PERSPECTIVES

What you see depends on where you are standing and the filter through which you are looking. There is no wisdom in asserting that your point of view or opinion is anything more than your current position and filter. It is the result of the narrative your mind delivers about what your senses perceive.

INSPIRATION
FOR TODAY
A little consideration, a little thought for others, makes all the difference.
Winnie the Pooh

Everyone is busily doing the same thing that you are: interpreting the world around them. The result is endless varieties of perspectives and filters. Choose a situation that you will be engaged in today and experiment with guessing what other people see and think about the same situation.

FLEXIBLE AND OPEN

The first step to a flexible and open relationship with life is to acknowledge that there are different ways of seeing the same situation. Without acknowledging that these different filters exist, it is practically impossible to experience openness to new understanding and wisdom. It is a beneficial exercise to try on the point of view that is opposite to the one you currently hold in any particular matter. Pick the thing you feel the strongest about and imagine writing a newspaper article from the opposite point of view, or imagine debating the opposite side of one of your favorite opinions.

The goal is to discover if you have enough flexibility to open up to other ways of thinking, without losing the integrity of your opinion.

What do you feel very strongly about?

NOTES

INSPIRATION
FOR TODAY
There is little difference in people, but that little difference makes a big difference. The little difference is attitude. The big difference is whether it is positive or negative.
W. Clement Stone

THE VALUE OF DIVERSITY

Activating community as a value in your life goes hand in hand with being willing to stretch beyond personal comfort zones. Sometimes the smallest differences, such as tastes in food, habits of culture, and patterns of speech can bring up enormous emotional responses. Valuing diversity is a way of saying yes to the transforming power of facing that which is unlike yourself and carefully watching your internal dialogue as you encounter that which you do not prefer.

How is it possible to coexist with people whose values are different from yours?

INSPIRATION
FOR TODAY
A difference of taste in jokes is a great strain on the affections.
T.S. Eliot

THE INNER KNOWING

Deep within you lies the Inner Knower. It speaks to you through intuition. Learn to separate its voice from the "monkey mind," chatter so that you can hear its clear message.

The Inner Knower is *not* the inner critic. It is the voice that always speaks affirmatively and lovingly.

Stop the noise of your life long enough to hear the wisdom it is trying to convey. It will guide you directly to the highest good.

NOTES

INSPIRATION
FOR TODAY
*To believe your own
thought, to believe that
what is true for you in
your private heart is true
for all men—that is genius.*
Ralph Waldo Emerson
Self Reliance

THE DIVINE WHISPER

We have grown so accustomed to noise and chatter that many people can't stand to be quiet anymore. They have to have the television set on in every room or a radio blaring.

We are a society of multi-taskers. We talk on the phone, check emails and watch TV at the same time. Rarely do we stop long enough to be present in the *now* moment.

INSPIRATION FOR TODAY

If you want to capture someone's attention, whisper.

T.V. adverstisement

All of this noise and activity blocks the Divine Whisper. Take some time each day to sit in the silence and just listen. You'll be amazed at what you hear.

GUIDANCE

There is no place on earth holier than others. The Presence of God is equally distributed throughout every location in the universe. The ground you walk on is holy. Wherever you go to be alone with God is your holy place.

Before you ask the advice of friends or the counsel of clergy, seek first the guidance of Spirit. Go to your holy place to be alone with Spirit and ask your question. And then give it time to answer. Listen closely for new ideas or intuitions.

Where is your holy place? If you don't have one, where could you create one?

NOTES

INSPIRATION
FOR TODAY
Holy ground is not
a place of pilgrimage:
it is where you are
when God finds you.
Peter J. Gomes

May 29

STILLNESS

We find Spirit in the stillness. When we stop the "monkey chatter" of our minds long enough to listen, we will hear The Voice.

Movement creates friction. Friction creates noise. Noise creates confusion. Non-movement creates stillness. Stillness creates receptivity. Receptivity invites The Presence of Spirit.

INSPIRATION
FOR TODAY
Be still and know
that I am God.
Bible Psalm 46:10
King James Version

Be still!

QUIET THE MIND

When our spiritual needs are not fulfilled, we develop desperate cravings because we are starved. Excess in behavior comes from having no peace in the mind. It is frenetic, chaotic and destructive.

Quiet your mind and peace will be restored. When peace is established, normality returns and cravings disappear.

What are you craving? What spiritual need has not been fulfilled?

NOTES

_____

_____

_____

_____

_____

_____

INSPIRATION
FOR TODAY

The natural person desires without craving and acts without excess. By not doing, everything is done.
The Tao

_____

_____

_____

_____

_____

_____

PEACEFUL EMOTIONS

NOTES

The heart has its own wisdom which the mind often does not understand. One isn't more valuable than the other. They are meant to be used in conjunction with one another.

Balancing mind and heart brings a powerful wisdom. One without the other is like a three-legged chair. It cannot stand on its own.

INSPIRATION
FOR TODAY
It is only with the heart
that one can see rightly;
what is essential
is invisible to the eye.
Saint-Exupery
The Little Prince

What brings peace to your heart? How do you achieve balance between what your heart feels and what your mind thinks?

INTUITION

What used to be called, "women's intuition" is not limited to just women. There is an Intelligence within us that communicates through intuition, thought and feelings. To capture its wisdom and direction for your life, you must listen.

Listening requires a conscious effort to slow down and stop the everyday noise of life. Create a space in your day to be still and listen. You will be amazed at what you already know.

NOTES

INSPIRATION
FOR TODAY
*The only real valuable
thing is intuition.*
Albert Einstein

June 2
LIFE IS A DANCE

A couple dancing find a point of transcendent beauty when there is a relationship of sufficient trust that one can lead uninhibited and the other follow unquestioning. If both dancers attempt to lead, there is likely to be frustration. If both are followers, who knows what will happen?

INSPIRATION
FOR TODAY
*Happiness, that grand
mistress of the ceremonies
in the dance of life, impels
us through all its mazes
and meanderings,
but leads none of us
by the same route.*
Charles Caleb Cotton

Imagine that your life is like a dance, more specifically, a dance with Life and that the moment of transcendent beauty comes when you sufficiently trust Life to lead you. Imagine closing your eyes and following as Life leads you along your own particular journey.

What would life be like if you started each day with an expectation of being guided through the mazes and meanderings of life by an expert lead?

THE LONG AND
WINDING ROAD

The path that meanders and seems to double back upon itself can be seen from a different perspective when enough distance is placed between the viewer and the view. From a distance, the long and winding road evens out, and the destination becomes obvious.

Have there been turns in your life that have taken you in a seemingly opposite direction from the purpose you had in mind? If so, how did it work out? If not, how would you advise someone whose life path seems to be meandering?

NOTES

_____

_____

_____

_____

_____

_____

_____

_____

_____

_____

_____

_____

_____

_____

_____

_____

INSPIRATION
FOR TODAY
The long and winding road
that leads to your door/
Will never disappear. /I've
seen that road before, it
always leads me here./
Leads me to your door.
Paul McCartney

June 4
SPIRIT GUIDED

NOTES

Built into the condition of being human is freedom. It sometimes seems easier to follow precise instructions than it does to sift through the information around us, picking up this hint from nature, this fact from science and this opinion from philosophy and then sitting with it all until a course of action reveals itself. But this is the gift of creation, that Spirit guides us without imposing.

INSPIRATION
FOR TODAY
Men give advice;
God gives guidance.
Leonard Ravenhill

Creation is so beautifully made that Its presence is everywhere. So when you want to access Spirit's guidance, you don't have to go anywhere special, other than to a place in your own awareness where you listen for the guidance from within your own silence.

KEEPING MY OWN COUNSEL

Listening to your intuition means having adequate quiet time that is undisturbed by other input such as opinions of friends and loved ones, advertising or entertainment.

Try this. Really slow down for a half hour and give yourself over entirely to the moment as if there is absolutely nowhere else you need to be and nothing else you need to be doing. Don't tell anyone else what you are doing and why. Grant this to yourself so that you are creating an intimate point in time where you are willing to deeply listen to your intuition.

Keep a pen close at hand and be willing to write down any thoughts, ideas or impressions that come your way. Don't be concerned if none of it makes sense. Don't even consult with anyone about what comes through to you. It might take a while, even days, before you reach clarity on what the moment revealed to you. But if you don't take that private moment, you'll never know.

NOTES

INSPIRATION
FOR TODAY

*Listen to your intuition.
It will tell you everything
you need to know.*
Anthony J D'Angelo

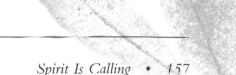

QUIET STRENGTH

Regular practice of quietness develops personal strength and self confidence. In the beginning, you don't even have to have a specific program or mental process to engage in. It is sufficient to set aside time for quiet stillness. Even fifteen minutes of quiet stillness daily has an accumulative effect and can create in you the resource with which to see the world around you as it really is. Over a span of years, regular quietness can develop serenity and tranquility in a world that you may not always understand. Above all, it is in quietness that you discover the door that opens to your intuition, and there is where God is.

Today may be a good time to ask for guidance from your own intuition and to listen with focused attention to what comes as the answer. Being as quiet and as motionless as you can, try to become aware of your heartbeat. After a while, ask yourself, "What do I need to be aware of today?"

INSPIRATION
FOR TODAY
*Nothing splendid has
ever been achieved except
by those who dared believe
that something inside
them was superior
to circumstance.*
Bruce Barton

DWELL THERE

Becoming aware of your intuition can be enhanced by consciously noticing the messages of life. To do this effectively you might experiment with reducing the noises and distractions of day to day activities on a regular basis. You might want to consider taking a closer look at the places you spend most of your time and evaluate how much unnecessary mental clutter is present. For example, American families have the television on between eight and eleven hours a day and many have more than one TV. Some families leave the radio or TV running in the background as a kind of ambient noise.

It must be very difficult to notice what life is saying if your dwelling place is a space of constant sound and stimulation. Of course, it's possible that Life's messages present themselves through everything and anything. What is the noise of your environment telling you? Maybe its telling you to take a break?

NOTES

INSPIRATION
FOR TODAY

There is always music amongst the trees in the garden, but our hearts must be very quiet to hear it.
Minnie Aumonier

June 8

FOLLOWING
MY INTUITION

NOTES

How does a person know what the voice of intuition is? How do you discriminate between the voice of inspiration and the voice of your cultural fears or ambitions? Learning to tell them apart is a lifetime's work. There are few clues along the way, which is why listening for Intuition is something worth practicing.

INSPIRATION
FOR TODAY
Trust your own instinct. Your mistakes might as well be your own, instead of someone else's.
Billy Wilder

American philosopher Ernest Holmes wrote that Intuition is God in humankind. With that as a starting point it might be worthwhile to consider that the voice of Intuition will never criticize you or ask you to do something dangerous to yourself or to others. It might challenge you to stretch your comfort level, but it will not use comparison or meanness as a motivation.

What do you think the voice of Intuition is?

LIVING IN THE NOW

This very moment is the only moment you have. To be fully present here and now requires conscious effort and attention. It means letting go of your plans for the future and forgetting the past. Very few people live that consciously. You can be one of them.

With practice, you can train yourself to be more present in the *now* moment. Centering your attention requires focus and discipline. But it is the greatest gift you can give to yourself. Being present where you are right now allows you to make better choices and decisions. When you are awake and present, you are truly alive!

Practice being present. When you're with a friend or loved one, give them your full attention. Listen when they speak. Don't multi-task or plan what to say in response. Just listen!

NOTES

INSPIRATION
FOR TODAY
Life is now.
There was never a time
when your life was not
now, nor will there ever be.
Eckhart Tolle
The Power of Now

June 10
PAYING ATTENTION

What are you giving your attention to? Wherever you place your attention, that's where Creative power is at work in your life. That's why people who think about, talk about and worry about their health always manifest disease quicker than anyone else. That's also why people who think about, talk about and plan for success always succeed.

INSPIRATION
FOR TODAY
You have to pay a lot of attention to what's important, what's permanent, what's real.
Jim Balsille

Your attention is *powerful*! It creates your future experience. That's why its very important to consciously select what you give it to. Here are some suggestions:

Think about what you like about yourself. Look at what you want to see manifest in your life. Talk to successful people and find out what they know. Concentrate on the good qualities in other people. Give your time and attention to the people you love the most.

MESSAGES FROM LIFE

You are not alone. You never have been. You are in the Presence of God every day. Everywhere you turn, God is sending you little messages. If you listen closely, you will hear God speaking through the waitress in the coffee shop. If you open your eyes, you will see the Holy artwork in the sunset. If you listen closely, you will hear God singing to you in the sounds of nature.

Open your eyes. Open your ears. Look around. Listen.

NOTES

INSPIRATION
FOR TODAY
The handiwork of God can be seen all around us…
Rumi

June 12
REDUCING THE NOISE

NOTES

_____

_____

_____

_____

_____

_____

_____

_____

_____

_____

_____

_____

_____

_____

_____

W here there is no friction, there is no noise. Noise is unwanted sound. It annoys us and causes stress. The body becomes tense, the mind unsettled.

In order to hear your spirit, you must stop the noise. You must go into the silence and experience the peace and quiet of a still heart.

INSPIRATION
FOR TODAY
Where the river is deepest,
it makes less noise.
Proverb

Notice the language of the universe. It makes no noise. It is silent. God doesn't speak out loud. When you know the truth, you don't have to defend it or argue for it. God is Love. It isn't talking about love. It is *being* Love!

What is making too much noise in your life? How can you reduce it?

Where do you go to be in the silence? How often do you visit?

MARVELOUS HAPPENINGS

I love the word "marvelous" because it reminds me to marvel over life; to keep my sense of wonder and awe. The Bible says that to enter the kingdom of heaven we must become as little children. This means we must live in a constant state of wonder and amazement.

As we grow older, it's easy for us to become cynical and jaded. But we must resist the ugly pull downward of the world and let our spirits soar freely as they did when we were children.

What is happening in your life right now that is marvelous? What marvelous people do you know? What do you marvel at?

INSPIRATION
FOR TODAY
*In all things of nature
there is something
of the marvelous.*
Aristotle

June 14
NEW POWER

NOTES

To seek power just for power's sake is to be ego-centric. To strategize for power or prestige is a futile effort.

Real power comes from knowing the truth. It rises up from within. Real power is internal power, not external. It can't be given to you, nor taken from you. It is an arrival point in awareness; a destiny of consciousness.

INSPIRATION
FOR TODAY
Nearly all men can stand adversity, but if you want to test a man's character, give him power.
Abraham Lincoln

Your position or possessions do not bring you power. Your title or education does not guarantee power. Your power comes from within. It comes from knowing your Source is God.

Connecting with that Source regularly will cause you to feel powerful. A new sense of authority will rise up from within. Doubts and fears will melt away and you will no longer be afraid to stand alone.

BEING MINDFUL

Living mindfully is about being present to what's going on around you and within you. Mindful living is capturing every moment whether it is joyful or painful. It means facing every issue head on and living without regrets.

Mindful people do not collect or store negative thoughts or feelings to use against others in the future. They express who they are, where they are. They don't try to hide. They use their minds for life-affirming ideas. They allow their hearts to feel every emotion without judgment or self-condemnation.

What regrets do you have? What has been left uncommunicated to others? What can you do now to clean it up?

NOTES

INSPIRATION
FOR TODAY

*My religion is to live and
die without regret.*

Milarepa

June 16

A HEALTHY PACE

There is nothing wrong with moving fast. And, there is no one-size-fits all solution when it comes to finding the pace that is right for you in different areas of your life. Nevertheless, it is useful to check in with yourself and ask about the pace you have chosen to live at and assess whether or not it contributes to peace of mind, balance and health.

INSPIRATION
FOR TODAY

Who forces time is pushed back by time; who yields to time finds time on his side.
The Talmud

SIMPLIFY, SIMPLIFY, SIMPLIFY

Henry David Thoreau gave the world enormous amounts of inspiration, a good portion of which encourages us to be aware of the beauty in every moment. He wrote, "A man's interest in a single bluebird is worth more than a complete but dry list of the fauna and flora of a town." And he reminded us that we are rich only in proportion to the number of things that we can afford to leave alone.

As you move through today, try to notice what the world has for you to see and experience.

NOTES

INSPIRATION
FOR TODAY
Alas! How little does the memory of these human inhabitants enhance the beauty of the landscape!
Henry David Thoreau

June 18

ONE THING AT A TIME

I learned a technique called TRAF for cutting through office clutter. Although I cannot remember the publication or who wrote it, I have never forgotten TRAF. The technique calls for doing one thing at a time and limits your options to Tossing, Referring, Acting, or Filing. I was impressed by the simplicity of the approach and how it created peace in the workplace for me. I applied TRAF to a paper-crowded desk, taking only one piece at a time and either tossing it, referring it, acting on it or filing it. Slowly the desk shifted shape before me and the overwhelming pile melted under the power of doing one thing at a time.

From time to time I remember that experience in the office and apply it with equally good results in other areas of my life.

Where might you benefit from doing one thing at a time?

INSPIRATION
FOR TODAY
It is not how much you do,
but how much Love
you put into the doing
that matters.
Mother Teresa

DO LESS, BE MORE

Have you ever spent an entire day alone, doing very little, and not speaking at all? If you have, perhaps you had the experience of being substantially refreshed afterwards. When I take a good period of time to do less, I find that it stimulates creativity and reawakens my attunement to the messages and inspiration of the world around me.

Perhaps taking a whole day off is not practical in your life at this moment in time. A similar effect can be achieved by reducing the number of tasks, contacts and conversations you agree to in your time off. Weekends, evenings and early mornings are great opportunities to practice doing less activity so that you can listen to the fascinating inner world of your intuition.

NOTES

INSPIRATION
FOR TODAY
Let us be silent,
that we may hear the
whispers of the gods.
Ralph Waldo Emerson

June 20
TURN IT OFF

When the doors of a commuter plane close just before preparing to take off, cabin attendants announce to the passengers that all electronic devices must be turned off. What follows is a period of relative peace—if you like flying—as the craft ascends past 10,000 feet, uninterrupted by ringing, beeps and messages.

INSPIRATION
FOR TODAY
*As you simplify your life,
the laws of the universe
will be simpler, solitude
will not be solitude, poverty
will not be poverty, nor
weakness weakness*
Henry David Thoreau

I've often thought of this instruction to turn everything off as something that would be of great benefit as a spiritual practice. A luxurious moment in which you are uninterrupted and inaccessible as you rise in spiritual altitude. And not only during spiritual practice...what other times in your day could benefit from turning some technology off? TV, radio, cell phone, iPod, pager, DVD, etc. When would less of these create more time for you to be available to your intuition?

BE STILL

The final pose in a hatha yoga practice session is called shavasana, or the corpse. This curious name is given to the pose because of the complete cessation of all outer movement other than involuntary processes such as breathing. Out of this intentional outer quietness, a profound inner quietness follows.

It's not the only way to be still inside, however for those who find it a challenge to calm the thought, it's worthwhile to try this: sit very still for 15 minutes and don't try to accomplish anything other than utter stillness. Make note of your experience afterwards, paying special attention to any thoughts or feelings that seemed to offer wisdom or guidance.

NOTES

INSPIRATION
FOR TODAY
In the midst of movement and chaos, keep stillness inside of you.
Deepak Chopra

June 22

SLOWING DOWN

Sometimes you have to speed up and sometimes you have to slow down. Life is complex and diverse and requires some flexibility in speed. Some folk have mastered "fast" and haven't practiced "slow." Both speeds are subjective and difficult to assign absolute values. However, you know what slow means to you. Today, experiment with going slower. Whenever you think to do so, say to yourself. "Slower."

INSPIRATION
FOR TODAY
Slow down and enjoy life.
It's not only the scenery
you miss by going too fast
—you also miss the
sense of where you
are going and why.
Eddie Cantor

Paradoxically, people who practice slowing down frequently report that their sense of engagement and accomplishment increases with the slower speed. Not only that, with slowness comes the invitation to notice the roses, and to eventually slow down enough to smell them also. It is in moments such as these that life waits to reveal something to those who are willing to pause.

I AM WILLING TO HEAR

I've heard it said that in any partnership, if both parties agree all of the time, one is unnecessary.

Your goal shouldn't be to surround yourself with people who agree with everything you say. No one learns anything new when that's the case. Having differences of opinion is healthy and creates a learning environment if people really listen to each other.

Do you really listen to people who think differently than you? Are you willing to hear criticism? Are you ready for the truth, even when it's uncomfortable for you to hear it?

Whose opinion do you value the most? Who will tell you the truth, no matter what? When you are faced with a challenge, do you go to that person first?

NOTES

INSPIRATION
FOR TODAY
Things can turn out the way you want, if you're willing to hear the truth.
T.D. Jakes

June 24

I KNOW WHAT TO DO

NOTES

There is a place within you that is absolutely clear. It is an inner place of perfect wisdom. It is the place where God resides within your soul.

When you are faced with confusion and are unclear as to what to do next, go to that place. Say to yourself, "When I don't know what to do, something in me does. And that something is revealing itself to me right now." Then be open to what wisdom rises to the surface. Go on about your day and listen for intuitions. The very thing you needed to know will become known to you.

INSPIRATION
FOR TODAY
Every time you don't follow your inner guidance, you feel a loss of energy, loss of power, a sense of spiritual deadness.
Shakti Gawain

TELLING THE TRUTH

If you really love someone, you mustn't be afraid to tell them the truth, even if it temporarily hurts their feelings or offends them.

The truth, though not always popular, is nonetheless the only thing that sets us free. It takes a courageous person to tell the truth, especially if you know it won't be well received. Telling the truth is always an act of love. It is loving someone enough to want what's right for them, even if it risks total rejection.

Honesty is the foundation for any quality relationship. Without it, you don't really have a relationship. What you have are two acquaintances who occasionally lie to each other.

NOTES

INSPIRATION
FOR TODAY
*I love you, and because
I love you, I would
sooner have you hate me
for telling you the truth
than adore me for
telling you lies.*
Pietro Aretino

THE POWER OF WISDOM

Having more information may grant you knowledge, but it will not guarantee wisdom. There are a lot of educated people in the world who lack wisdom. And there are very wise people who lack education. The two do not necessarily go hand in hand.

Wisdom comes from knowing Universal Truth; that which is true for all people under any circumstance. Here are examples of Universal Truth:

INSPIRATION
FOR TODAY
What we're learning in our schools is not the wisdom of life. We're learning technologies, we're getting information.
Joseph Campbell

What you send out returns back to you.

You can only attract what you are.

You cannot receive anything you're not first willing to give.

Everything changes. Nothing in this world is permanent.

Love is the reason you exist and the only thing worth living for.

STAYING ON COURSE

We each must follow the beat of the drum we hear. Sometimes, others can hear the same drum as we do and so we travel the path together. Other times, we alone hear the drum and others have to depart our company to follow their own destiny. On such an occasion, it is important to remember that we are all individuals who travel separate paths to the same location.

If the course you are on leads to greater love, joy or ease, then stay on it. If it does not, get off the path you're on and rejoin your soul's destiny to greatness.

All paths converge at some point and lead to the same destination. We come from Spirit, so we must all eventually return home to Spirit, with our own tales to tell about our journey.

NOTES

INSPIRATION
FOR TODAY
*If a man does not keep
pace with his companions,
perhaps it is because
he hears a different
drummer. Let him step to
the music he hears, however
measured or far away.*
Henry David Thoreau

DISCERNMENT

NOTES

People communicate who they are and what they believe in a million different ways. Rarely does the mouth reveal the truth. It is through the actions of a woman or man that their beliefs reveal themselves.

When you meet someone new, don't listen too closely to what they say. Just watch what they do. That will tell you who they are. Actions really do speak louder than words.

INSPIRATION
FOR TODAY
Look at the means which a man employs, consider his motives, observe his pleasures. A man simply cannot conceal himself!
Confucius

They may have a mountain of excuses to help rationalize their behavior, but most of the time people do what they really want to do. That's why it's so easy to see who they are if you just observe their actions.

How do your actions communicate what you believe?

AGREEING WITH LIFE

There are certain spiritual principles that govern life in the universe. They cannot be taught to people. They must be discovered over time and through personal experience.

Once you capture the wisdom that resides within you, life gets a lot easier. You can avoid a lot of pain and suffering. Dysfunctional relationships get healed and love becomes the number one priority.

Eventually you realize it's a lot easier to go with the flow of life than to try to fight it. Agreeing with life means letting go of ego agendas in favor of God agendas.

NOTES

INSPIRATION
FOR TODAY

We cannot teach people anything; we can only help them discover it within themselves.
Galileo

June 30
THE WAY I SEE OTHERS

NOTES

When you look at other people, what do you see? Or, in other words, what are you telling yourself about them? Some people frequently compare themselves to others, making a mental list of favorable and/or unfavorable qualities in themselves and in others. Using this information, they paint a mental picture of the person that is based largely on opinions that may or may not be accurate.

INSPIRATION
FOR TODAY
*Those who never retract
their opinions love
themselves more than they
love truth.*
Joseph Joubert

Today, when you notice that you're beginning to formulate a story about a person you're interacting with, consider asking yourself, "Is my opinion about this person accurate?" Then try to imagine how someone who loves this person would describe them to you.

THE WAY I SEE MYSELF

The words "wholeness" and "healing" are related. It is no coincidence that an attitude of healing is frequently accompanied by an awareness of wholeness. Applying this to how you see yourself means accepting all of yourself. This is the key to a healing attitude of mind. When you mentally review yourself, what aspect of yourself do you have difficulty accepting? Being willing to lighten up a bit on those areas that may be hard to accept is a helpful starting point to developing a healing attitude. Maybe today's journal entry can begin with "I am willing to lighten up about..."

NOTES

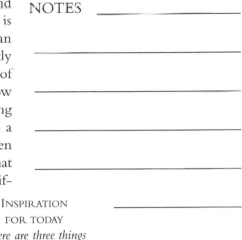

INSPIRATION
FOR TODAY
There are three things extremely hard: steel, a diamond, and to know one's self.
Benjamin Franklin

MIRROR IMAGE

Activating healing in life is the same as cultivating an awareness of wholeness. To assist you in this, life has conveniently surrounded you with reflective surfaces: everybody and everything is reflecting back to you some thought, feeling, or attitude that you have. To use the mirror effectively requires paying attention to what your mind thinks it sees. Try this:

INSPIRATION
FOR TODAY
*Life is a mirror and will
reflect back to the thinker
what he thinks into it.*
Ernest Holmes

Whenever your mind tells you something about what your eyes see—such as "She is beautiful" or "He is sarcastic"—try to come up with at least three examples of how this is also true of you.

How are you beautiful? How are you sarcastic? This is a way to begin developing a consciousness of wholeness.

I LOVE MYSELF

NOTES _____

The word "cherish" means to treat with affection and tenderness, to hold dear. Try that with yourself. Can you? How would it change the way you go through today?

_____

_____

_____

_____

INSPIRATION
FOR TODAY
*Cherish all your happy
moments: they make a fine
cushion for old age.*
Booth Tarkington

_____

_____

_____

_____

July 4
I RESPECT MYSELF

NOTES

The word "respect" means to regard with honor or esteem. Try that with yourself. Can you? If you were to show respect for yourself today, what would change as you move through the day?

INSPIRATION
FOR TODAY
Self-respect is the fruit of discipline; the sense of dignity grows with the ability to say no to oneself.
Abraham J. Heschel

THE WAY GOD SEES ME

It is an interesting exercise in perspective to assign human attributes to the Divine so that I can imagine or try to imagine how God would be in various human situations. For example, what would a God's-eye-view be? C. S. Lewis wrote, "What seem our worst prayers may really be, in God's eyes, our best." These words remind me to be expansive when I'm assigning human attributes to God. In other words, when imagining God looking at a particular situation, I wonder if He or She has to wade through cultural conditioning, preferences, fears and ambitions. There is no real answer to this question, but it is helpful to imagine that when the Divine looks at you, It sees without the filters through which I see. Perhaps all It sees is the truth. Or maybe It sees everything: creed, culture, height, weight, history and preferences, etc., but in addition, It sees your soul, for want of a better word. Perhaps practicing to see in this way is not a bad idea at all.

NOTES

INSPIRATION
FOR TODAY
If any of you lacks wisdom, let him ask of God, who gives to all liberally and without reproach, and it will be given to him.
James 1:5
New American Standard

HEALTHY SELF-IMAGE

NOTES

A healthy or wholeness-oriented self-image neither skips over shortcomings nor over emphasizes them. It doesn't overstate positive elements, nor does it avoid mentioning them out of false humility. A healthy self-image is all inclusive, forgiving and realistic.

Here is a great exercise: describe yourself as a novelist would when introducing a new character in the story, with a balanced attention to character flaws and strengths.

July 7

BODY/MIND CONNECTION

There is no separation between the body and the mind. They are in equal partnership in service to the Whole.

Every thought creates a biological response that is immediately acted out in your body. By changing what you habitually think, you can reshape and reform your body.

You have unlimited power at your disposal. Whatever your mind can conceive can be achieved.

NOTES

INSPIRATION FOR TODAY

Judging from accounts of mystical experience, heightened creativity, or exceptional performance by athletes and artists, we harbor a greater life than we know. There we go beyond those limited and limiting patterns of body, emotions, volition, and understanding that have been keeping us in dry-dock. Instead we become available to our capacity for a larger life in body, mind, and spirit. In this state we know great torrents of delight.
Jean Houston

July 8

MY BODY RESPONDS TO MY MIND

You are not a victim of genetics or environment. You are the co-creator of your own fate. Your body responds to faithful and directed thought.

Each day, give loving consideration to the miracle of your body. It is a master machine created to house your spirit. There is an intelligence operative within it that knows how to sustain it in health.

Think life-affirming thoughts and you support that intelligence in maintaining the health of your body. Think negative thoughts and you disrupt the natural flow of ease and create conditions that invite disease.

You are the co-creator of your body. Use your thought, wisely.

INSPIRATION
FOR TODAY
Men at some time are masters of their fates: The fault, dear Brutus, is not in our stars, but in ourselves, that we are underlings.
Act I, Scene II.
Julius Caesar
Shakespeare

I LOVE AND NURTURE MY BODY

When you look in the mirror, what do you say to yourself? Is it something kind and considerate or mean and hateful?

Because we receive so much negative input from our society about our bodies, it's difficult for some to learn to love them.

Maybe you're on a diet right now. Maybe you're not happy with the way you look. Whatever the case, it's still important to love your body as it is.

Here's a hint to get you started: Find something you like about your body. Do you have great eyes? Do you have strong shoulders or beautiful hands? Any part of your body that you like is your starting point. Now, concentrate on that part until your like turns to love. Keep looking at what you like and your affection will grow. It may seem simple but it's a great way to start loving your body.

What new ways can you find to love and nurture your body?

NOTES

July 10

THINKING MAKES IT SO

William James wrote: "The greatest discovery of my generation is that human beings can alter their lives by altering their attitude of mind." He is quoted as saying, "If you change your mind, you can change your life." I have found it to be true, but not always easy; we can change our lives by changing our thinking—in both directions, for good or for bad. Just the simple shift away from dwelling on resentments or rerunning bad scenes from the past has made a significant shift in my mood and as a result in my actions.

INSPIRATION
FOR TODAY
She that fails to command
her thoughts will soon lose
command of her actions
Unknown

Denis Waitley expressed it like this: "Our limitations and success will be based, most often, on your own expectations for ourselves." And Frank Outlaw, perhaps the most elegantly of all, said it like this: "Watch your thoughts; they lead to attitudes. Watch your attitudes; they lead to words. Watch your words; they lead to actions. Watch your actions; they lead to habits."

HARMONIOUS LIVING

When what you think, say and do are in harmony with each other, you are living an authentic life. With no conflict between thought and action, you live as an example to others of true leadership.

Harmony begins in the mind. All contradictions must be resolved there before harmony can be established. A mind that is teeter-tottering between thoughts of self-love and self-degradation cannot be at peace. All negative thoughts must be met and dissolved in mind first. Questions of value have to be answered. Fears and doubts must be resolved in your mind so that balance and harmony can be restored.

Harmony is not bestowed upon us. It doesn't fall down from heaven. It is worked for and maintained with diligence through regular and mindful self-examination. It requires discipline and persistence.

NOTES

INSPIRATION
FOR TODAY
Happiness is when what you think, what you say, and what you do are in harmony.
Mahatma Gandhi

July 12
FLOW

Life is like a river that flows in one direction, and you are standing in the river. You have a choice: you can try to resist the flow of the river and swim upstream. If you make this choice, you will eventually grow weary and exhausted. Or, you can choose to go with the natural flow of the river.

INSPIRATION
FOR TODAY
Life is a series of natural and spontaneous changes. Don't resist them—that only creates sorrow. Let reality be reality. Let things flow naturally forward in whatever way they like.
Lao Tzu

Our frustration comes from trying to make things happen that aren't ready to happen. Our sorrows come from trying to hold things together that really should come apart.

Allow the natural flow of life to carry you downstream. Enjoy the ride. Take in the sights and keep an open mind. The river will take you to unplanned destinations and surprise you with unexpected gifts.

HEALTHY PHYSICAL BEING

Health is natural. Disease is unnatural. Health is permanent. Disease is temporary. Health is your birthright. Disease is a man-made invention created by fear of separation from God.

God does not use illness or suffering as a teaching tool. Disease does not come from any agenda of Spirit.

If you are not feeling well, remind yourself that nothing of value is obtained in suffering through illness. No good is gained that couldn't be received in a more positive experience.

Renew your mind with the truth and your body will respond in health.

NOTES

INSPIRATION FOR TODAY

Disease is not a power over you. It has no agenda for your life. It has nothing to teach you. You do not improve in any way by suffering through it.
Chris Michaels
Your Soul's Assignment

July 14

I ATTRACT LIKE-MINDED PEOPLE

NOTES

When I first heard the phrase "I attract like-minded people," I thought it to be a fine description of how things work in life. I began to look at the people around me and wondered to myself how it was that I had attracted all of them.

Then I began to look forward to using this idea and asked myself, "What kind of like-minded people am I interested in attracting more of?" I thought of qualities such as generosity, loyalty, and kindness. Then it became clear to me that I had just given myself what has turned out to be a lifelong assignment: to develop these qualities in myself so as to be attractive to like-minded people. "I attract like-minded people" is not only a description of how life works...it can be a mission, a creative endeavor and a hobby, if you choose it.

INSPIRATION
FOR TODAY
We do not attract what we want, but what we are.
James Lane Allen

FUNCTIONAL AND WHOLE

Activating healthy relationships in your life requires wisdom. Wisdom is about wholeness and the ability to hold opposing ideas and allowing differences to coexist. Healthy relationships depend on your commitment to embrace the whole, seeing how every person has a part to play.

NOTES

INSPIRATION
FOR TODAY

Wisdom is your perspective on life, your sense of balance, your understanding of how the various parts and principles apply and relate to each other. It embraces judgment, discernment, comprehension. It is a gestalt or oneness, an integrated wholeness.
Stephen R. Covey

July 16

LOVING CONNECTIONS

When we get caught up in the busy pace of our lives, it is possible to lose connection with one another. Not only do we risk losing connection with the people who are important to us, but we risk losing connection with the everyday people we engage with in ordinary life activities.

INSPIRATION
FOR TODAY
*A hidden connection
is stronger than an
obvious one.*
Heraclitus of Ephesus

Not every encounter has to be a heart connection and not every person we interact with becomes a best friend. However, since we do interact with people all of the time and our paths do cross, why not allow these ordinary instances to be loving? Not in an obvious or overly demonstrative way, but rather like simply trying to remember to look at the people who cross paths with us and pay mindful attention to them.

GROWING AND HEALTHY

B ritish novelist and play-wright David Story is quoted as saying, "The essence of true friendship is to make allowances for another's mental lapses."

I take these words to heart, and I'm grateful for the many times close friends have turned a blind eye to my blunders. I'm grateful that they have patiently allowed me to grow from the person I was into the person I'm becoming. Their patience has helped me to be patient with myself and has taught me not to lose sight of the love that brought us together in the first place.

Some of the most precious memories are of friends who care enough to tell me what they see that I cannot. Typically, they are the same people who cared about me and believed in me when I could not care about or believe in myself.

Whose council are you grateful for in your life?

INSPIRATION FOR TODAY

It is one of the severest tests of friendship to tell your friend he's false. So to love a man that you cannot bear to see a stain upon him, and to speak painful truth through loving words, that is friendship.
Henry Ward Beecher

FAMILY

_____

_____

_____

_____

_____

_____

_____

_____

_____

_____

_____

_____

_____

There is no need to fix yourself, your family or your friends. People are people wherever you find them, and wherever you find people, there you will also find all of the interesting frailties and curiosities that come with being human.

Try making a list of all the members of your family and under each person's name, list their strongest qualities. It might be that the best thing you can come up with is that they are usually punctual. Good! Or it might be that they are generous and caring in a way that you admire. Good! Let today be about looking for the best in your family, no matter what. If you do not have family, pick your closest friends for the same exercise.

INSPIRATION
FOR TODAY
*He that has no fools,
knaves, nor beggars in his
family, was begot by a flash
of lightning.*
Thomas Fuller

FRIENDS

Someone said, "If you want to have a friend you must first be a friend." What does being a friend mean to you? What are the qualities in a person that make the difference between their being an acquaintance and being your friend? What are the top three most important qualities to you in friendship? And finally, are you an embodiment of those qualities?

NOTES

INSPIRATION
FOR TODAY
*Friendship with oneself
is all important because
without it one cannot be
friends with anybody else
in the world.*
Eleanor Roosevelt

HEALTHY RELATIONSHIPS

NOTES

I have no control over my best friends. I have no desire to control any of them. My delight comes from experiencing them, their choices, decisions, and lives. I feel privileged to witness them. I noticed that whenever I try to influence them or pressure them to do or be something, a stressful change emerges, and too much stress is not healthful.

INSPIRATION
FOR TODAY
A friend is someone who lets you have total freedom to be yourself.
Jim Morrison

Stress happens a lot when I want friends to be different in some particular way. I may not be one hundred percent successful when I try to not interfere. However, the healthiest relationships I have are with those I accept most freely.

MONEY IS SPIRIT IN FORM

Money is a means to an end. It represents the flow of good into your life. It was designed to create freedom and ease in your life. It represents the spiritual Law of Circulation and flow.

In order for money to serve you well, it must be used with wisdom and love. Like all good things, it is not meant to be hoarded in fear. It is supposed to be put into circulation.

Here is the best formula for using your money: Give some, save some and spend some—in that order! That will keep it in circulation and ensure that more returns to you.

Do you believe that money is a good thing? Do you believe that God wants you to prosper? How do you use your money to support what you believe?

NOTES

INSPIRATION
FOR TODAY
Money is good!
Money is God in action!
Eric Butterworth
Spiritual Economics

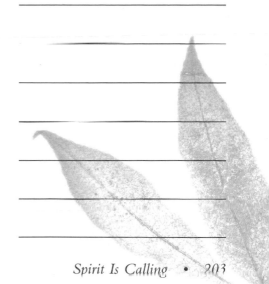

July 22
DEBT FREE

Overspending and over-charging on credit cards has become a major addiction for many people. It is a vicious cycle that keeps them trapped in living from paycheck to paycheck. As with all addictions, the only solution is to completely abstain from use.

If you are overspending, today is the day to end the cycle. Cut up your credit cards right now! Get help from a credit counselor or financial planner and start living on a cash basis. It's hard to do at first, but the long-term benefits are tremendous. The sense of freedom from debt is overwhelming. It's like taking a five hundred pound monkey off your back.

INSPIRATION
FOR TODAY
Credit buying is much like being drunk. The buzz happens immediately and gives you a lift.... The hangover comes the day after.
Joyce Brothers

Kin Hubbard said, "Who recalls when folks got along without something if it costs too much?" Break the cycle of our consumer-addicted culture. You don't have to buy the latest gadget just because it's advertised on television.

MORE THAN ENOUGH

There is more than enough air for everyone to breathe. There is more than enough love for everyone to feel and enough health for everyone to have. The universe is filled with an abundance of all good things. But each of us can have only what our consciousness will allow.

Raise your expectations of what life can offer you. Expect to prosper from every venture. Expect to be liked by every person you meet. Expect new opportunities to show up daily. Lift up your eyes from the ground and see the vastness of space. You are surrounded by infinite abundance!

NOTES

INSPIRATION
FOR TODAY
The world is full of abundance and opportunity, but far too many people come to the fountain of life with a sieve instead of a tank car…a teaspoon instead of a steam shovel. They expect little and as a result they get little.
Ben Sweetland

ABUNDANCE

You have a responsibility to manifest the glory of God's abundance. The more you love, the greater the world can be. The more you prosper, so shall those around you also prosper. The greater health you experience, the greater joy you express. As you are lifted up, so are those around you.

INSPIRATION
FOR TODAY
It is not only my right and my privilege to walk in the abundance God has for me, it is my responsibility...
Jan Denise

You have a duty to live the best life you can conceive of living, thereby providing the world with a good example of a life well lived and a person well loved.

LOVE'S OFFERING

Love brings us opportunities to grow whether we are prepared for them or not.

Love breaks all boundaries and overcomes every prejudice. It is *not* convenient. In fact, love is very inconvenient. It's not supposed to fit into your comfortable schedule. It is supposed to take you out of your schedule.

Love heals all things that are broken. It is the only thing of real value in our lives.

NOTES

_____

_____

_____

_____

_____

_____

_____

_____

_____

_____

_____

_____

_____

_____

_____

INSPIRATION
FOR TODAY
Can there be a love that does not make demands on its object?
Confucius

July 26
PLEASURE TO GIVE

NOTES _____

_____

_____

_____

_____

_____

_____

_____

_____

_____

_____

_____

_____

INSPIRATION
FOR TODAY
*There is no happiness
in having or getting,
only in giving.*
Henry Drummond

You are not in this life to make a withdrawal. You are here to make a deposit. There is something of great value you have to give to life; something unique and powerful. Your gift can change the world. It can lift someone's spirit. It can save a life.

Your perspective matters. Your words are powerful. Your wisdom transforms. Your love heals.

You have many gifts that you're unaware of. Think about what you have to give the world. Make a list of the gifts you can give.

HEALTHY FINANCES

inancial health means having enough money to do what you want to do, when you want to do it. Like the health in your body, it requires attention and discipline.

Know your financial worth. Don't live in denial of how much you owe. Be clear on the market value of your assets. Create a financial plan that will fulfill your vision of living prosperously.

What can you do today to ensure you will live well in the future?

NOTES _____

_____

_____

_____

_____

INSPIRATION
FOR TODAY
I've been rich and I've been poor; believe me, honey, rich is better.
Sophie Tucker

_____

_____

_____

_____

_____

_____

_____

_____

July 28

I AM HONEST

NOTES

On the surface, honesty is about stating the facts as best as you believe them to be. However, activating honesty as a pathway to spiritual understanding requires an in-depth look at how you see the world and how you come to believe things.

An excellent place to begin is to explore the meaning that you give to everything in your world. As an experiment, try to slow down enough in your thinking today to notice the meaning that things have for you, whether you're noticing a pain in your hand or a tree in the garden. It is possible that this exercise will lead you to a place where you realize just how little you honestly know about the origin of your beliefs. This is a wonderful and liberating place to begin an exploration of honesty.

INSPIRATION
FOR TODAY
Truth fears no questions.
Unknown

HONEST TO GOD

In his book *Honest to God*, John A. G. Robinson wrote, "God is, by definition, ultimate reality. And one cannot argue whether or not ultimate reality really exists. One can only ask what ultimate reality is like..."

Discovering what reality is like may seem at first to be easy, even obvious. However, on closer examination it is possible to discover that we see what we want to see and don't see what we don't want to see. And among the things and events we do see, what we are dealing with first is the narrative we create to describe what we see. Sometimes, that narrative gets in the way of what is really before us.

Use Paul Tillich's phrase, "the creative ground of all being" to imagine that everywhere you go, you are immersed in reality and that all you have to do today is to look into reality and meet it exactly as it is, without any assistance from your ability to create meaning.

NOTES

INSPIRATION
FOR TODAY
*Be cautious of people
who are very certain
about what they know.*
Edward Viljoen

MY NEW LIFE

NOTES

The word "sincere" comes from Latin, sine cera, which means "without wax." Apparently, there was a time when artisans would hide the faults and cracks in cheap pottery and marble by pressing in wax so that they could get a higher price than was honest. Imagine a devotional marble statue on the mantelpiece above the fire, revealing its flaws with the heat from the fire below. Sculptures and pottery became stamped "Sine Cera" to assure that they were of good quality, with no fillers.

INSPIRATION
FOR TODAY
*Sincerity is the highest
compliment you can pay.*
Ralph Waldo Emerson

This is a powerful idea for activating honesty in your life. Approach your day today without any filler. Notice when you're smiling at someone and you don't mean it. Notice when you say you'll call or keep in touch, but you have no intention to do so. Notice when you agree with someone, but your heart isn't in it.

I MUST TRUST

Of course, you don't have to trust! However, chances are that you've already tried that as an approach to living. The problem is that with or without trust, life continues in just the same way.

NOTES

INSPIRATION
FOR TODAY
*Our greatest glory is not in
never falling, but in rising
every time we fall.*
Confucius

August 1
HONORABLE

NOTES

_____

_____

_____

_____

_____

_____

_____

_____

_____

_____

_____

_____

_____

_____

_____

What if somebody found this journal and read all your writing? Make some notes about thoughts in this journal that are truly private and belong to you and make some notes about the thoughts that need to be communicated to the people in your life.

Not everything needs to be expressed, especially if you haven't yet spent time investigating whether or not it is true. And there is an emotional intelligence in you that will assist you in knowing when there is something that you are thinking and feeling that would be better to share with the person(s) involved.

INSPIRATION
FOR TODAY
Truly, to tell lies is not honorable; / but when the truth entails tremendous ruin, / To speak dishonorably is pardonable.
Sophocles

MY CORE VALUES

Make three lists: 1. What people value about me the most is... 2. What I value most in other people is... 3. What I think people should value the most is...

After you've made the list, look for values that appear in all three lists. When this exercise works, it can reveal the values that are most important to you in your life. You can use the values that are common to all three lists as a focus for noticing when you are in alignment with them and when you are not.

NOTES

INSPIRATION
FOR TODAY
The secret of a good life is to have the right loyalties and hold them in the right scale of values.
Norman Thomas

August 3
BEING HONEST

NOTES

_____

_____

_____

_____

_____

_____

_____

_____

_____

_____

_____

_____

_____

_____

_____

_____

Being honest with yourself sometimes requires sorting through a lifetime of acquired thoughts, attitudes and beliefs. You may need to investigate which are really true and which are not. Being honest with yourself in this way gives you the best chance of being honest with others. You can start anywhere, anytime, with anything or anyone.

INSPIRATION
FOR TODAY
*Set up as an ideal
the facing of reality
as honestly and as
cheerfully as possible.*
Dr. Karl Menninger

After an encounter, pause for a moment and ask yourself what you thought about it. Writing your thoughts down is very helpful because it slows down your thinking. Then take a moment to look at your thoughts on paper and ask yourself, "How much of this is realistic and true?" And then ask yourself, "Is this how God would report the situation?"

COURAGE TO TELL THE TRUTH

The truth starts with your having the courage to tell yourself the truth. It means shining a light on all areas of your life where you have been in denial.

Many people avoid asking themselves simple questions that could lead them to a happier life. Questions such as: Am I happy with who I am? Do I love my job? Am I still in love with my spouse/partner? They avoid asking those questions, because they don't want to be truthful. They'd rather pretend they don't know the answers and live in denial.

Get real! Be honest with yourself. And then make whatever changes you need to make to restore joy and peace to your life.

NOTES

INSPIRATION FOR TODAY

The naked truth is always better than the best dressed lie.
Ann Landers

August 5

LOVE ENOUGH FOR TRUTH

_____

_____

_____

_____

_____

_____

_____

_____

_____

_____

_____

_____

_____

_____

Are you more attached to your opinion or the truth? When you advise others, do you think about what is best for them, or what you think they should be doing?

The greatest gift of love is to be present for another person, without needing anything from them. Being there to serve them in any way you can without wanting anything in return is of immense value.

INSPIRATION
FOR TODAY
Often what we think is best for others is distorted by our attachment to our opinions: we want others to be happy in the way we think they should be happy. It is only when we want nothing for ourselves that we are able to see clearly into others' needs and understand how to serve them.
Mahatma Gandhi

FALLING IN LOVE
WITH THE TRUTH

We seek universal truth—that which is true for all, under any circumstance. We are tired of opinions and false judgments. We want the whole truth, and nothing but the truth. That which we seek, we shall find.

When we fall in love with the truth, we are unwilling to settle for anything less.

Lies told for centuries don't make them any truer. Institutions built around false doctrine have no validity, no matter how long they have been standing.

Life is all about sorting out the truth from the lies.

NOTES

INSPIRATION
FOR TODAY
*Rather than love,
than money, than fame,
give me truth.*
Henry David Thoreau

August 7
CLARITY

On a dark summer night in the midst of a storm, when the sky is pitch black, suddenly a flash of lightening lights up the entire horizon—and for one brief moment of clarity everything can be seen. And then as quickly as it came, the moment is lost; the darkness returns and we are left with a brief memory of perfect vision.

INSPIRATION
FOR TODAY
Children are remarkable for their intelligence and ardor, for their curiosity, their intolerance of shams, the clarity and ruthlessness of their vision.
Aldous Huxley

Life is just like that summer storm. We have moments of perfect vision, then months of confusion. In some areas of our lives we are crystal clear, and in others totally blind. This is true for everyone. That's why a true friend is the one who sees for us what we can't see for ourselves. We rely on their clarity and hang on to them tightly, like a blind person does a sighted one.

Who sees for you when you are unclear? Do you return the favor?

BUILDING TRUST

There are a number of questions that must be resolved in your mind before you can learn to trust. They are:

Is there a God? Is there something at the helm of this universe directing it towards some purpose? Is God good? Is God's plan one that brings greater life, ease, love and joy? Does God want all that's good for *me*? Does God want me to succeed and be happy, or have I been excluded somehow?

Answer these questions for yourself and you will learn to trust. The answers cannot be found in a book or an institutional doctrine. Look within!

INSPIRATION FOR TODAY

To believe in God for me is to feel that there is a God, not a dead one, or a stuffed one, but a living one, who with irresistible force urges us towards more loving
Vincent van Gogh

August 9

EMOTIONAL TRANSPARENCY

It is a mistake to think that vulnerability is a weakness. The truth is that being open demonstrates great strength. Openness and receptivity invite the richness of life and allow you to be fully present to beauty and love.

Be willing to sit with emotions without judgment or condemnation. Don't try to fix them or hide them. Just allow them to be what they are.

INSPIRATION FOR TODAY

When we were children, we used to think that when we were grown-up we would no longer be vulnerable. But to grow up is to accept vulnerability... To be alive is to be vulnerable.
Madeleine L'Engle

Emotions were designed to emote, as an outward expression of your soul's feelings for the human experience. There is no right or wrong, good or bad emotion.

Think of a time when you tried to hide or suppress what you were feeling. How did it affect you? What were the results?

THE FOUNDATION OF TRUST

Trust is necessary to life. It is as basic as eating and breathing. We trust our bodies to assimilate our food. We trust the sun to rise each morning and set each night. We trust that we will wake up again tomorrow morning. We live by faith in the unseen and the unknown everyday. To trust is to be open to life, to accept it's vulnerabilities and remain steadfast.

The alternative is to not trust and that cannot be an option. To trust no one closes you off. It builds an impenetrable wall around you. You are left alone, trapped inside.

Don't be afraid to trust.

NOTES

INSPIRATION
FOR TODAY
*You can't shake hands
with a clenched fist.*
Indira Gandhi

August 11

BALANCING TRUTH
WITH KINDNESS

Telling the truth is a powerful tool in activating spirituality. And the style in which the truth is told can add to or detract from the effectiveness of spiritual practice. I heard someone say of an acquaintance that she wielded truth like an axe. I hope I will never be remembered like that.

INSPIRATION
FOR TODAY
*The end result of kindness
is that it draws people
to you.*
Anita Roddick

The fact is, this description was true of me at one time. So I began making an effort to learn how to balance truth telling with kindness. I have since found that kindness will guide me in what style of words to use when truth telling. Kindness will not let me off the hook, however. As an agent of love, kindness has moved me to say difficult things to loved ones. But not before it demanded of me a careful review of my intention, attachment, and perception.

Good luck!

COMPASSIONATE COMMUNICATION

Compassionate communication means that you have an interest in the impact of your communication, in particular as it relates to relieving suffering of any kind. This becomes interesting when the communication you are about to make contains bad news. How do you tell somebody that they didn't make the team when they have been dreaming about that appointment for years?

Mindfulness means paying attention to the person to foster a sense of shared experience. This can be achieved by asking questions about the person's feelings or even details about the person's life. Give yourself some time to mentally and emotionally prepare for the communication so that you are not distracted by your own needs and discomforts. Taking time means not rushing through the communication, and allowing silence to be part of the compassionate exchange. Choose an environment for compassionate communication that ensures there are no unnecessary distractions or interruptions, such as telephone calls.

NOTES

INSPIRATION
FOR TODAY
*The most important thing
in communication is to hear
what isn't being said.*
Peter Drucker

August 13

PURE INTENTION

NOTES

It is possible for words to say one thing, while facial gestures and body language say something else. It is also possible for words to say one thing outwardly while the inner meaning is something different. Purifying your intentions means that you attempt to say no more and no less than what you actually mean. This can be particularly helpful when you find yourself thinking that somebody should understand what you mean without your having to say it. You might find yourself trying to say something with your posture or facial expression while your words say something else.

INSPIRATION
FOR TODAY
It's amazing how much you can learn if your intentions are truly earnest.
Chuck Berry

Today, try to pay attention to what your body and your face express and keep note of whether or not that matches your words.

226 • *Spirit Is Calling*

GENTLE AND KIND

In your opinion, who is the gentlest and the kindest person who is alive or who has ever lived? What about them is gentle and kind? How do they treat people and talk to people? Imagine that you had an audience with that person and enough time to ask anything you wanted. What would you want to know and what do you imagine their answer would be to your question?

NOTES

INSPIRATION
FOR TODAY
If you want others to be happy, practice compassion. If you want to be happy, practice compassion.
Dalai Lama

August 15
LOVE IS FEARLESS

NOTES

I remember vividly a time when my brother fell and hit his head. I had always been terrified of blood and anything that had to do with injury and pain. Nevertheless, all of my fear and my instinct to run vanished the instant I realized he needed me. I walked to him calmly as if I knew exactly what to do and how to do it.

INSPIRATION
FOR TODAY
*There is a power for good
in the universe, and you
can use it.*
Ernest Holmes

FEAR IS LOVELESS

Fear is an inherent human reaction that can help us avoid dangerous situations. However, reactions of fear can be learned or acquired as the result of upsetting incidents, or inherited from the beliefs of your family of origin. Certain fears are more common than others within a culture, and sometimes people learn these fears without questioning them or without ever having experienced the situation feared.

When thinking of the things you fear, which of them are beyond your control to change?

NOTES

INSPIRATION
FOR TODAY
*No one can rob us
of our own soul.*
Ernest Holmes

A SPOONFUL OF SUGAR

NOTES

When Mary Poppins sang "A spoonful of sugar makes the medicine go down…" the message was clear: It helps to be nice. Journalist Mignon McLaughlin said it this way: "Don't be yourself. Be someone a little nicer." Unfortunately, the word "nice" has strayed in meaning from its original sense of being pleasant and kind. Today, it is often associated with behavior that is overly friendly or ingratiating, and "sweet" can be used as a term of dismissal. But there is a different kind of nice, and a different kind of sweet that contributes to the smooth and beautiful workings of the world. It's the nice that is your original innocence and the sweet that is your genuine kindness.

INSPIRATION
FOR TODAY
*Behave so the aroma of
your actions may enhance
the general sweetness
of the atmosphere.*
Henry David Thoreau

To get in touch with innocence and kindness, make a list of the people in whose presence you feel like smiling. Or, make a list of people whose voices calm you. Or make a list of people who ignite kind feelings in you.

CLEANING OUT THE CLOSETS

Letting clutter accumulate in your house, car or garage creates a block in the Law of Circulation. If you want to open your life to greater good, take what you no longer use and give it away to someone who can use it. Or sell your old possessions and bank the money. Getting rid of stuff that you no longer use opens the flow of spiritual energy back to you.

Start with your closet. Get rid of everything you haven't worn in the past six months or year. Get rid of the clothes that no longer fit. Get rid of the "guilt clothes," the ones you spent too much money on but don't really like anymore. It's okay to let them go. You'll be amazed at how much lighter you feel when you clean out the clutter in your life.

NOTES

INSPIRATION
FOR TODAY

Your possessions are spiritual energy, given to you to use and care for. When certain things are no longer necessary to your experience and you allow them to remain in your life, you create stagnation in the flow of spiritual energy.
David Owen Ritz

August 19

CONFIDENCE AND DIGNITY

We all reach that point of authority in our lives; that place where we can no longer stand pretending to be something we're not, just to please other people. That is the point of power in our lives; a personal declaration of independence. It's also the point in your life where you finally accept yourself, just as you are.

INSPIRATION
FOR TODAY

There comes a time when you have to stand up and shout: This is me damn it! I look the way I look, think the way I think, feel the way I feel, love the way I love! I am a whole complex package. Take me...or leave me. Accept me—or walk away! Do not try to make me feel like less of a person, just because I don't fit your idea of who I should be and don't try to change me to fit your mold.
Stacy Charter

No human being is perfect. We all have flaws. And yet, greatness and genius are also within us. We are capable of so much love and compassion.

Accept the whole package, the things you like about yourself and the things you want to change. Declare your independence from other people's opinions and judgements. Be your own woman or man!

FREEDOM FROM GUILT

You are doing the very best you can with the wisdom you currently possess. Given what you know, you are making the best decisions you can make. This is true for all of us.

Self-forgiveness is required to release guilt. That doesn't mean you make excuses for poor behavior or choices. It is not a rationalization for knowingly hurting someone. It is an admission that if you had known better, you would have done better. Given what you knew at the time, you made the best choice you could have made.

To release guilt, start with self-forgiveness. And if appropriate, ask for forgiveness from the person who was affected by your behavior.

What guilt do you carry around with you? What can you do to release it?

NOTES

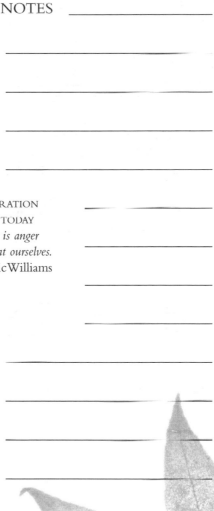

INSPIRATION
FOR TODAY
*Guilt is anger
directed at ourselves.*
Peter McWilliams

NO MORE SHAME

NOTES

There is a moral compass at the center of every soul, knowing which choice is right and which is wrong. When we are in touch with that place inside ourselves, we are guided to right choices, ones that lead to life-affirming results. When we are not, just the opposite occurs.

Do not fear your own self-expression. Speak your mind. Tell your story. Let your genius out. You have been created with a unique perspective on life that no one else has. Until you say it, it hasn't been said. Until you write it, it hasn't been written.

INSPIRATION FOR TODAY
We but half express ourselves, and are ashamed of that divine idea which each of us represents.
Ralph Waldo Emerson

AS I AM

The Intelligence at the helm of the universe does not make mistakes. It is a perfect Intelligence (God) that only knows perfect pattern. You are its amazing creation. You are an individual identity of its Spirit. There is nothing you can't do, given your partnership.

Never hide what God has made. You are who you are by the specific choice and design of your Creator. Let out what God has made by being exactly who you are, without shame or fear.

NOTES

INSPIRATION
FOR TODAY

The universe must exist for the self-expression of God and the delight of God.
Dr. Ernest Holmes

THIS IS ME

Stop pretending to be something you're not. Stop hiding. Give the world the full dose of your spirit and wisdom.

Stop trying to gain approval from others. When you approve of yourself, they will get in line to approve of you as well. Until then, your self-value will teeter-totter based on their false judgment and opinion.

INSPIRATION FOR TODAY

I must be myself. I cannot break myself any longer for you, or you. If you can love me for what I am, we shall be happier. If you cannot, I will still seek to deserve that you should.
Ralph Waldo Emerson
Self Reliance

Trust that what God created you to be is good enough. Let go of your fear of rejection and step out into the fearlessness of full expression.

Stop defending or justifying your life. It's okay if people don't understand you. Many great people have been misunderstood. Jesus was misunderstood. Socrates was misunderstood.

Stop doubting your abilities. They have been given to you by God. Let your talent loose on the world and glorify your Creator.

NOTHING TO HIDE

ove is the most powerful force in the universe. It lives as a burning desire inside you, demanding your soul's fullest expression. It will not let you rest until you fully expose your unique self.

Love will not allow you to hide, or to live in fear. It will broadcast your true thoughts and feelings in a million different ways so others will eventually see. You cannot hide your real self. Inevitably, who you are must come out.

NOTES

INSPIRATION
FOR TODAY
*Love makes your soul
crawl out from its
hiding place.*
Zora Neale Hurston

August 25
A SOUL OF INTEGRITY

NOTES

Your soul operates with complete integrity whether or not you do. It knows when a lie is being told, even if you've got yourself and everyone around you fooled. It is a wonderful and inspiring thought to know that your soul knows exactly what is going on.

INSPIRATION
FOR TODAY
*At some point you stop,
and looking back, you
realize you knew, and
you've always known.*
Edward Viljoen

TRANSPARENT

S tress reduces when transparency increases. Transparency doesn't necessarily mean that you share every detail of your life with everyone. It does mean that there is integrity in your thoughts, intentions, words and actions. It means that to the best of your ability you are what you say you are, you mean what you say, and you do what you commit to doing.

Does this seem too high a standard for living? Well, consider the alternative. Consider the price we pay for not being authentic. It takes a tremendous amount of precious life energy to maintain an image that is out of sync with reality. It takes a lot of mental resources to keep on top of words, stories and actions when they are out of sync with your soul.

A good place to begin exploring transparency is by examining your motives for doing a thing. When you have the opportunity, ask yourself, "Are my motives easily seen and understood by others?"

NOTES

INSPIRATION FOR TODAY

Life is filigree work. What is written clearly is not worth much, it's the transparency that counts.
Louis-Ferdinand Celine

August 27
AUTHENTIC

Before you get in touch with your authenticity, it is a good idea to learn how to be quiet and to spend time with yourself. It's a good way to discover exactly what your authenticity is all about. With the endless sounds around us, the messages of advertising and the ever-present nag of cell phones, email and schedules, it's easy to lose track of what and who you really are.

INSPIRATION
FOR TODAY
The authentic self is the
soul made visible.
Sarah Ban Breathnach

Many people have discovered that by being quiet, they can find something within that is warm and sincere, true and genuine. And it takes a little practice. It's like dating—so at first you might have to be patient, even gentle, with yourself.

To get started, try answering these questions without editing your answers. Who are you? What do you do in the world? How do you manage the important tasks in your life? What is the reason you do what you do?

LIVING FREE

Sometimes in life we rush forward from event to event as if we have no choice in the matter. Sometimes the rushing is so intense that we miss the down-to-earth satisfaction in simple things such as breathing, drinking, chewing and just being. Maybe you really do have a busy schedule. But is there a possibility that in your thinking, you remain free to focus and experience in any way you want? Maybe today you could go about your business, fast-paced or not, and exercise your freedom to slow down your attention. Try carrying a bag of carrots, raisins, or nuts around with you. Whenever you feel the rush of life pulling you forward, exercise your freedom to pop a treat into your mouth for the purpose of having an ecstatic moment of enjoyment. Chew and enjoy. Taste before you swallow. Let the world linger on "pause," and do not hurry to finish.

What in your schedule today do you have to do, and what do you not have to do?

NOTES

INSPIRATION FOR TODAY

The secret of happiness is freedom. The secret of freedom is courage.
Thucydides

August 29
NO MORE LIES

NOTES

People spend a lot of time managing the way other people see them, sometimes even fooling themselves into believing their own presentation. A study published in the Journal of Basic and Applied Psychology found that sixty percent of people in an experiment lied at least once during a ten-minute conversation. From pretending to like something they actually didn't, to falsely identifying their career, they just managed the truth.

What, if anything, are you not exactly accurate about when communicating with other people?

INSPIRATION
FOR TODAY
A lie would have no sense unless the truth were felt as dangerous.
Alfred Adler

TRUTH WITHOUT EFFORT

Telling the truth may not always be easy; however, it gets easier with time. As you practice telling the truth, balanced with kindness, over time you will develop effortlessness in telling the truth. You'll develop a sense for when you need to pause to do your own inner reflection, and when it is time to open your heart and share your experience in an undefended way. Contributing to effortlessness in telling the truth is the ability to hear what another person says in response to your sharing.

You've read these questions before. Try them again: Who will tell you the truth, no matter what? When you are faced with a challenge, do you go to that person first?

NOTES

INSPIRATION
FOR TODAY

If people only knew how hard I work to gain my mastery, it wouldn't seem so wonderful at all.
Michaelangelo
Buonarroti

August 31

THE TRUTH SHALL
SET YOU FREE

NOTES _____

_____

_____

_____

_____

_____

_____

_____

_____

_____

_____

_____

_____

_____

Is there something in your life that needs to be addressed? Perhaps a communication that is long overdue? An apology? A thank you note? Is there a debt owed you that is overdue? Do you have unfinished business?

INSPIRATION
FOR TODAY
*The time is always right
to do what is right.*
Martin Luther King, Jr.

SERVICE

How are you using your time here on earth? Are you using all of your assets for yourself and a small circle of friends and family?

What do you have to offer the world? What do you have to give that will make a difference to someone you will never know? How can you leave the world better than you found it?

At the end of the day, do you feel that what you've done with your time and talent has added value to someone's life? Do you have a genuine sense of fulfillment?

By answering these questions, you will learn something about yourself and how you are living your life.

INSPIRATION FOR TODAY

Only those who have learned the power of sincere and selfless contribution experience life's deepest joy: true fulfillment...
Anthony Robbins

NOTES

_____

_____

_____

_____

_____

_____

_____

_____

_____

_____

_____

_____

_____

September 2
COMMUNITY

There is only *one* human community in our world. We belong to each other. We have been placed here to love and care for each other by our Creator.

We are responsible for what happens to all of our children, not just our biological offspring. Every time a child dies of starvation in a third-world country, some part of us dies with them. Every time a violence occurs, it scars every soul, including the perpetrator.

INSPIRATION
FOR TODAY
Isn't everyone a part of everyone else?
Budd Schulberg

We pretend that we are separate to guard our hearts from breaking. We ignore the hardship and struggle of others to avoid taking responsibility. We tell ourselves that one person can only do so much, so we have an excuse for doing nothing.

MY CONNECTION LIFE

You are a link in a chain of causation that stretches behind and in front of you for thousands of generations. Your actions, thoughts and choices affect everyone and everything in that chain.

Separation is an illusion. We are all connected on a spiritual level. We share the same DNA, though it is assembled in a unique pattern in each individual.

An intricate web of Life connects everyone to everything and every-thing to everyone.

You are not alone. You never have been. You are permanently connected to every soul that has ever lived. And we are all connected to God.

INSPIRATION
FOR TODAY
The life I touch for good or ill will touch another life, and that in turn another, until who knows where the trembling stops or in what far place my touch will be felt.
Frederick Buechner

September 4
SELF-FULFILLMENT

Because we are all connected, service to others is really service to ourselves. By giving what we have to each other, we become self-fulfilled.

There is no greater satisfaction than the feeling that what you said or did helped change someone's life for the better. As we reach to lift someone else up, we too are lifted up.

INSPIRATION
FOR TODAY
The sole meaning of life is to serve humanity.
Leo Tolstoy

It is a mistake to try to gain self-fulfillment through ego pursuits. If you satisfy your ego with no regard for others, you will find yourself alone with your riches and still lonely. Your successes will be meaningless and shallow.

248 • *Spirit Is Calling*

GIVING TO OTHERS

It is overwhelming to consider the needs of the billions of people in our world. Problems exist in global proportions.

However that doesn't mean we can't begin to solve them right where we are. History has shown that one person with a clear intention and a bit of determination can indeed change the world. Ghandi is a good example. Dr. Martin Luther King, Jr. is another.

Take what you've got and give it to someone who needs it. Giving doesn't always have to be monetary. You have love to give. You have encouragement and wisdom to give. You have kindness and compassion. You can give a listening ear, or an open heart. You can give forgiveness and acceptance.

If everyone would give something good each day, we could transform the world.

NOTES

INSPIRATION
FOR TODAY
*If you can't feed a hundred
people then just feed one.*
Mother Teresa

September 6

TOGETHER WE ARE STRONG

NOTES

If two similar plants are put together in the same pot, their roots intertwine and grow together, giving each one greater strength than either would have had alone. This same truth applies to people as well.

Nature draws us to people of like mind because what we can accomplish together exceeds what any of us can do alone. All successful partnerships are based on this principle.

Who gives you strength and encouragement? Who do you empower?

INSPIRATION
FOR TODAY
*The whole is greater than
the sum of its parts.*
Unknown

ACTIVATING SERVICE

The world can't wait any longer. It is in desperate need of the few courageous people who are willing to give something good to it. The world needs people who know how to love and be loved back. It needs people who know how to give and receive blessings in return.

Be the one to make a difference. Decide today to start giving what you've got to others and watch your whole life be transformed before your very eyes.

NOTES

_____

_____

_____

_____

_____

INSPIRATION
FOR TODAY
How wonderful it is that nobody need wait a single moment before starting to improve the world.
Anne Frank

_____

_____

_____

_____

_____

_____

_____

_____

September 8
COMING FROM JOY

You may not be able to give as much as you want to the people and places you love. You may not be able to meet every need that exists in the world. You may not be able to achieve every goal you set for yourself in life.

You may not always be able to see the result of your service right away. It may not always be clear to you exactly how your contribution affects anything. You may find that, at times, your generosity is low and you don't feel quite up to hearing about the needs of even the closest of friends. From time to time, you may lose confidence and wonder if it is wise to give anything at all.

Give yourself joyfully anyway, and watch what happens.

INSPIRATION
FOR TODAY
Your gift of love, time, or service may not be received in the way you had hoped for. Give it freely anyway.
Edward Viljoen

UNCONDITIONAL GIVING

Use nature as your guide in this matter. Notice how it gives: Without condition. Whether or not you or I appreciate it, or receive it, Nature gives. It gives in lavish abundance whether or not anyone thanks it. And Nature keeps on giving even when it is not valued or cherished.

There is a difference between giving for the sheer joy of giving, versus giving for the purpose of receiving acknowledgment, thanks, appreciation. Giving for the sheer joy of giving is how Nature gives. It's natural.

How do you give?

INSPIRATION
FOR TODAY

But groundless hope, like unconditional love, is the only kind worth having.
Unknown

September 10

NON ATTACHMENT

NOTES

Activating service as a spiritual value is one of the fastest and surest ways to explore how attached you are to being recognized, acknowledged, or thanked. Service is the spiritual practice in which we confront the reality that we have absolutely no assurance that our gift of time and effort will be received as intended. A service-oriented mind requires maturity and an awareness of self worth that does not depend on acknowledgment.

INSPIRATION
FOR TODAY
Attachment is the great fabricator of illusions; reality can be attained only by someone who is detached.
Simone Weil

Serve because your soul understands your part of the whole and be free from the results of your contribution. Let service be about your own soul's integrity. It's deeply personal. It's about your desire to express life.

THE GREATER GOOD

Cells in the human body do not work for themselves. Neither do organs. Everything works together to maintain the integrity of the whole body. For the elbow to be successful in what it does it depends on the cooperation and collaboration of every other part of the body.

Consider the clothing you're wearing right now. Who designed it? Who created the machinery and tools that produced it? Who raised the children who became the adults who had the idea to create such a garment? Nothing exists by itself.

How do you contribute to the integrity of the whole?

INSPIRATION
FOR TODAY
He who wishes to secure
the good of others, has
already secured his own.
Confucius

September 12

A LINK IN A CHAIN

NOTES

Oftentimes, independence and freedom are held high as ideals to pursue, and rightly so. However, without *interdependence* there can be no structure to uphold freedom. Interdependence is the energy of being responsible for each other, sharing values and agreements. When each individual is a link in a chain, each one has an equally important position in the upholding of the whole. William James expressed it this way: "The community stagnates without the impulse of the individual. The impulse dies away without the sympathy of the community."

In what way are you dependent on others? In what ways are others dependent on you?

INSPIRATION
FOR TODAY
*When we try to pick out
anything by itself, we find
it hitched to everything else
in the Universe.*
John Muir

OUT OF THE SPOTLIGHT

There are all kinds of ways to give service. Many professionals offer a portion of their professional time pro bono as a service to humanity. Others find that they benefit when they take a break from their regular vocation and discover service in something completely different from what they usually do. Imagine a high-tech professional serving in the soup line for example, or a teacher helping in a creek restoration project. Getting out of the light of their regular skills can help them access a service mindset in which they are free. Nevertheless, all forms of service are valid and valuable.

What kind of service calls to you? Consider whether you are doing it to get into the spotlight. That will help you decide if perhaps it's time for you to make a different kind of offering to the world.

NOTES

INSPIRATION
FOR TODAY
*We're all in this together,
by ourselves.*
Lily Tomlin

September 14

SERVING WITH HONOR

NOTES _____

_____

_____

_____

_____

_____

_____

_____

_____

_____

_____

_____

_____

_____

A ctivating honor in service simply means applying the same quality, respect, timeliness and effort in your service as if you were doing it for someone you truly value and respect, such as yourself or a loved one. A sure way of upholding honor in service is to keep your agreements and follow through as promised. Accomplishing this may require you to be more circumspect with what you agree to do.

INSPIRATION
FOR TODAY
A "no" uttered from the deepest conviction is better than a "yes" merely uttered to please, or worse, to avoid trouble.
Mohandas Gandhi

When you serve, do you apply yourself without reservation? Do you complete your agreements?

WORKING TOGETHER FOR GOOD

As a team we can accomplish more. Organize a team of people who are interested in making the world a better place to live. Find projects you can work on together. Support a cause that you are passionate about. Feel the energy that comes from accomplishing a goal together. That energy heals and blesses every member of the team.

We have enough sports teams. We need "change teams"—groups of people who come together to change the world and improve the quality of life on earth.

Who will be on your team? Who do you know that's passionate about making a difference in the world?

NOTES _____

INSPIRATION
FOR TODAY
TEAM—
An acronym meaning:
Together Everyone
Achieves More.
Unknown

September 16

PLAYING MY PART

Since you are a spiritual being, your purpose in life is spiritually based. It may have nothing to do with your career. In fact, it may be a calling that is far greater than any employment can offer.

To find your purpose, ask yourself these questions:

INSPIRATION
FOR TODAY
Your destiny lies within you. Your purpose can be found within your heart's knowing.
Chris Michaels

What have I always dreamed of doing?

What secret or private dream have I not shared with anyone?

What world issues or problems really disturb me?

What am I especially talented at doing?

What gifts do I have that would help others?

Where do I feel I could make the most positive impact?

COOPERATION

Process requires cooperation. No one accomplishes anything alone. Everything is a collaborative effort.

Through process, we learn about ourselves. We find our talent and our limitations. We learn to depend on others. We learn to trust in the unknown. Process builds community and bonds us together as One.

What are you trying to accomplish on your own? Who do you know that could help you? Are you willing to partner with them? If not, why not?

NOTES

INSPIRATION FOR TODAY

Process transforms any journey into a series of small steps, taken one by one, to reach any goal. Process transcends time, teaches patience, rests on a solid foundation of careful preparation, and embodies trust in our unfolding potential.
Dan Millman
The Laws of Spirit

September 18

TEAMWORK

NOTES

The ego wants to be acknowledged. It hungers to be fed. It loves trophies and certificates with your name printed in bold letters. The ego wants everyone else to know that it was *your* idea that was implemented.

Working together as a team is ego shattering. When no particular person gets the credit, ego agendas have to be set aside.

INSPIRATION
FOR TODAY
*It is amazing how much
you can accomplish
when it doesn't matter who
gets the credit.*
Unknown

Are you comfortable working with others as a team? How important is it for you to get the credit for what's accomplished?

COLLABORATIVE EFFORT

As the old saying goes, "Two heads are better than one." When we collaborate with others, we double our impact and intensify our efforts. Talents and gifts are shared in an environment that fosters creativity. New ideas are born.

What creative project are you working on that could benefit from someone else's talent?

INSPIRATION
FOR TODAY
Great discoveries and improvements invariably involve the cooperation of many minds. I may be given credit for having blazed the trail but when I look at the subsequent developments I feel the credit is due to others rather than to myself.
Alexander Graham Bell

September 20
FENG SHUI

Feng Shui is the Chinese philosophy that governs spatial arrangement and orientation in relation to patterns of yin and yang and the flow of energy to yield favorable effects. It is the art of placement and arrangement of objects in a particular space.

The metaphysical counterpart is to have everything in its rightful place in your life. Is your relationship with God in order? Are you in the "right space" with your family and friends? Are your finances in order? Do you know how much you owe?

INSPIRATION
FOR TODAY
A place for everything, everything in its place.
Benjamin Franklin

Putting things in order in our lives gives us peace of mind. When we know how things are, and where things are, life runs a lot smoother.

September 21

THE INTEGRITY
OF THE WHOLE

It is possible to go out on a limb and *not* fall. You can take a different path than the masses of "play-it-safers" and still maintain your spiritual integrity.

Inside your comfort zone is the usual. Outside is the extraordinary, the uncommon. Where do you prefer to live?

NOTES

INSPIRATION
FOR TODAY
Be daring, be different, be impractical, be anything that will assert integrity of purpose and imaginative vision against the play-it-safers, the creatures of the commonplace, the slaves of the ordinary.
Cecil Beaton

HEALTHY BOUNDARIES

Service is an act of putting other people and their interests first. However, you don't have to give up your entire schedule to perform selfless service. Even an hour of service a month contributes something wonderful to the world. Service is a way to express your soul's feeling of connection to the world around you and it does not demand that you give yourself away entirely to fulfill its mission. It is preferable that you begin your service with an attitude of openness and well-being and that you engage in service that you can truly feel harmonious about doing. With that in mind, it's okay to say "no," or "I've had enough." It is important that in the service, the server is nourished too.

INSPIRATION
FOR TODAY
I think it is important to set boundaries. Remember that working on a holiday is a personal choice and doesn't have to be the only option.
Jeff Rosin

WHAT IS MINE TO DO

Knowing what service to engage in has something to do with following your heart. It has something to do with paying attention to what you notice. Some people notice the homeless, whereas other people are drawn empathetically to matters that involve children, and still others feel the call to support single parents. Whatever it is that is yours to do, you have the possibility of doing it from your happiest frame of mind. When you serve in this way, the people and organizations that you're called to serve are receiving the benefit of your *highest* frame of mind.

NOTES

INSPIRATION
FOR TODAY

There is no duty we so much underrate as the duty of being happy. In being happy we sew anonymous benefits upon the world.
Robert Louis Stevenson

HEART VALUE

NOTES

Noticing what has "heart value" for you could mean paying attention to your feelings when you consider service opportunities you would like to engage in. The benefit of being attuned to your feelings is that it gives you an opportunity to gauge whether or not your contribution will be in alignment with your values. For example, a peace activist may notice that peace in the world has heart value for her. However, if her activism involves agitation and violence, she might experience a sense of being disconnected from her heart value which relates to peace. Similarly someone interested in human dignity might want to be certain that his engagement in service is deeply rooted in dignity rather than in pity.

INSPIRATION
FOR TODAY
But the eyes are blind.
One must look with
the heart...
Antoine
de Saint-Exupery

IN ALIGNMENT

The phrase "in alignment" makes me think of gears in machinery at work when they are properly positioned to meet each other in exactly the right place. The end result is movement. When the gears are not in alignment, the machinery's function is thwarted. I've seen the same thing happen when somebody comes into a group or organization and wants to help, but their ideas and efforts are not in alignment with the machinery of the organization. This can be something as simple as rushing in with many new ideas without taking time to learn what the organization needs and wants.

Service is the practice of putting the needs of an individual or organization ahead of your own. It stands to reason that before you step into service, you might want to learn about the values and mission of the organization or individual and listen deeply to what their needs are. That way, if you have what they're looking for, the gears fall into alignment and the machinery is helped forward.

NOTES

INSPIRATION
FOR TODAY
Just as your car runs more smoothly and requires less energy to go faster and farther when the wheels are in perfect alignment, you perform better when your thoughts, feelings, emotions, goals and values are in balance.
Brian Tracy

September 26
EFFORTLESSNESS

When is your participation in the world effortless? When there is nothing to prove, no one or nothing to change, I am guessing that a deep sense of joy comes from performing the service itself. If there is effort at all, it would be the energy used to redirect the thoughts and emotions towards a free-flowing letting go so that as you engage in your service, you can let your heart lead the way in what to say, what to do, and even what to think.

INSPIRATION
FOR TODAY
For the progress of humanity, work alone is not adequate, but the work should be associated with love, compassion, right conduct, truthfulness and sympathy. Without the above qualities, selfless service cannot be performed.
Sai Baba

TIME HONORED

Timing has something to do with paying attention as opportunities to contribute arise, and then seizing those opportunities without delay. In other words, trust the message of life around you, your intuition, to successfully bring to you the openings that will be of greatest value to your personal growth and to the well-being of whatever organization or individual you serve. This is a way of honoring the rightness of the time when your insight reveals itself to you.

NOTES

INSPIRATION
FOR TODAY
*Liberality lies less in
giving liberally than in the
timeliness of the gift.*
Jean de la Bruyere

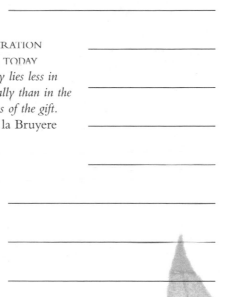

LEARNING TO SAY "NO"

Although learning to say no can seem difficult to some people, there are techniques that can help you become more at ease with the practice. It is especially difficult to say no if you think you are responsible for meeting the requests and expectations of every person who asks you for something. However, doing things that go against your idea of joyful service can easily contribute to a sense of unhappiness and feeling used.

INSPIRATION
FOR TODAY
Self-respect is the fruit of discipline; the sense of dignity grows with the ability to say no to oneself.
Abraham J. Heschel

Try being direct in your response by starting with no. Rather than beginning with an explanation, simply say, "No, I can't do that." Part of practicing no is giving yourself the right to request a delay in your answer while you review what you really want to say.

Another aspect is learning to say no to yourself when you want to say yes out of a sense of obligation.

RESOURCES TO DO WHAT I WANT

Rarely do we get exactly what we want, when we want it. But we always get exactly what we expect. Raising your level of expectancy is the best thing to do with your time. It takes discipline and persistence to build faith. But the results are amazing!

It's easy to say, "Expect great things to happen." But if you have a lot of past experience that says "Crap happens," it's difficult to start expecting good all of the sudden.

Work daily on your belief system. You can change your experience, one thought at a time. Let go of old beliefs in lack and limitation. Grab hold of new ideas of abundance and *don't let go*! Support your new belief system by reading materials and attending classes or workshops. Surround yourself with likeminded people who are working to lift up their beliefs as well.

If you do this, one day you won't have to work on it anymore. You will wake up and *expect* life to be good all of the time!

NOTES

INSPIRATION FOR TODAY

Expect your every need to be met. Expect the answer to every problem, expect abundance on every level.
Eileen Caddy

September 30
PLENTY OF TIME

NOTES

Everyone has the same amount of time in each day. Doing what you want in life has nothing to do with getting more time. No one can get more time. The same 24 hours is allotted to each of us. So, it's really a question of what you are giving your time to.

Experience teaches that people basically do what they really want to do. They take time, or *make* time, to do the things that are most important to them.

What are you spending your time doing? What takes up most of your time? What would you like to give more time to? Why aren't you doing it?

INSPIRATION
FOR TODAY
How we spend our days is, of course, how we spend our lives.
Annie Dillard

LOTS OF LOVE

Without love, life has no reason or meaning. It is vacant and cold. It has no depth or warmth. Love is the reason you are alive and the greatest reward for being alive.

Human relationships are a workshop for learning about love. They prepare us for a Love that transcends our bodies, unlimited by the separateness of human personalities. They allow us to see who we are, and what we really believe. They mirror our own strengths and weaknesses. They force our growth by challenging our capacity for patience, forgiveness and compassion.

To be blessed is to have a *lot* of people to love and who love you in return.

NOTES _____

_____

_____

_____

_____

INSPIRATION
FOR TODAY
Love doesn't make the world go round. Love is what makes the ride worthwhile.
Franklin P Jones

_____

_____

_____

_____

_____

_____

_____

_____

October 2
A PICTURE OF HEALTH

If you want to be the picture of health on the outside, you have to make sure the picture you have of yourself on the inside matches.

What do you think of yourself? Do you like your body? Do you say kind things to yourself when you see the reflection of your body in the mirror? What do you believe about disease? Where does it come from? What purpose does it serve? All of these questions must be resolved in your own mind before you can have a belief system that supports and sustains health.

INSPIRATION
FOR TODAY
As I see it, everyday you do one of two things: build health or produce disease in yourself.
Adelle Davis

The truth is that there is an Intelligence within you that knows how to sustain health. God is always your health-care provider. The Creator of the body knows exactly what is necessary to keep it healthy. But you partner with this Intelligence daily. What you eat, how you use, or abuse your body and what you think all contribute to your health.

A VITAL EXPERIENCE

To be a vital part of life, you have to find the courage to step away from the crowd and be yourself. We make our footprints alone. Together, we trample the ground. Don't be afraid to go your own way, dance your own dance and think your own thoughts. We are vital as we break through old boundaries and forge new paths, not by following the same footsteps that have gone before us.

Think about the last time you felt vital and vibrantly alive. I bet you were trying something you'd never done before.

NOTES

INSPIRATION FOR TODAY

There is a vitality, a life force, an energy, a quickening, that is translated through you into action, and because there is only one of you in all time, this expression is unique.
Martha Graham

October 4
LAUGHTER

Look around! People are hysterical. We are the funniest creatures on earth. There is a lot to laugh at.

Finding someone who "gets you," who laughs at the same things you do, is the greatest treasure on earth. Before you find something funny to laugh at, find someone to laugh with.

INSPIRATION
FOR TODAY
What soap is to the body,
laughter is to the soul.
Yiddish proverb

WHAT IS PROSPERITY?

Living a prosperous life isn't just about having more money. It also includes health and vitality, loving relationships, joyful expression in your work, and a strong relationship with God. Prosperity includes happiness, freedom, peace and ease.

The rich aren't rich because they have money. They have money because they are rich. They have a consciousness of prosperity that *causes* money to come to them and multiply. A prosperity consciousness is the cause and money is the effect. In other words, the rich are rich because of the way they think. Their thoughts and beliefs about prosperity cause an abundance of money to appear.

NOTES

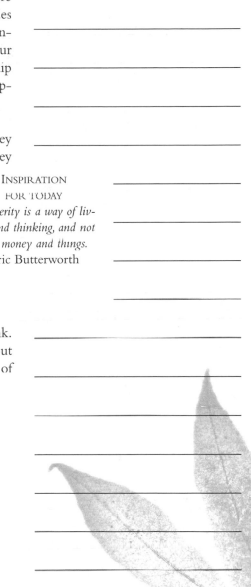

INSPIRATION
FOR TODAY
Prosperity is a way of living and thinking, and not just money and things.
Eric Butterworth

October 6

THE LAW OF CIRCULATION

NOTES

The best description I know of the Law of Circulation is in Luke 6:38: "Give, and it shall be given unto you in good measure pressed down, and shaken together, and running over...for with the same measure that Ye mete, it shall be measured to you again."

The message is simple: What you set in motion in life bears an uncanny resemblance to what comes around in your life. In particular, the scripture says that it is the measure (attitude) in which you do a thing that establishes the nature of the returning action. To me, "the measure" also means the awareness, or the motive underneath the initiating action—and that is what determines the nature of the result.

Are there exceptions to this rule?

> INSPIRATION
> FOR TODAY
> *Every happiness I enjoy,*
> *I attribute to my practice*
> *of giving.*
> Edward Viljoen

MY GIVING ATTITUDE

Giving is a wonderful practice, especially when you can give with an attitude of gratefulness. Being able to feel gratitude for the ability to give anything to anyone is what one of my teachers calls a high holy privilege. I try to think of giving as a way of expressing thank you. I am not always successful because sometimes my old attitudes of giving to get attention, or giving to get appreciation, or giving to get control creep in. But when I'm strong in my attitude of thankfulness, then my practice of giving is so very sweet.

NOTES

INSPIRATION
FOR TODAY
It is possible to give without loving, but it is impossible to love without giving.
Richard Braunstein

October 8
GIVING FREELY

NOTES

Eric Butterworth wrote, "A committed giver is an incurably happy person...a secure person, a satisfied person and a prosperous person." Over time I think I may have figured out why this is so from something Ernest Holmes taught about the nature of Love. He called Love "The self-givingness of the Spirit..." In other words, giving is God's Nature, and when I am giving, I'm duplicating that nature in my activity, and when I am not, it is as if I'm going against my own nature, and that's when it gets all blocked up and stagnant.

INSPIRATION
FOR TODAY
Giving frees us from the familiar territory of our own needs by opening a mind to the unexplained worlds occupied by the needs of others.
Opera Bush

WHAT GOES AROUND...

his is a clue to understanding the Law of Attraction.
It's not only what you do
that matters, it's how you do it. The
manner in which you give a gift,
for example, has everything to do
with the resulting activity generated by the giving. Another way to
say it is this: The spirit in which
you give makes all the difference to
your experience. For example, if
you give a little and your
motivating awareness is
to get a lot, you can be
sure that you are setting
in motion the creation of
people, situations or
organizations who give
you a little in order to
receive a lot from you.
("With the same measure that you
mete.")

NOTES

INSPIRATION
FOR TODAY
The love we give away is
the only love we keep.
Elbert Hubbard

October 10

SO SHALL YOU RECEIVE

There is wisdom to the words that warn us "Be careful of what you wish for, you may get it." Another way of expressing this is to say that our passion draws us to what we focus on. We may think our motives or desires are well hidden, and perhaps they are hidden from people around us. But your hidden desires are well known to you, and because they are, they play a significant role in how you show up in the world, and in what you allow to be welcome in your life.

INSPIRATION
FOR TODAY
God answers sharp and sudden on some prayers, / and thrusts the thing we have prayed for in our face, / a gauntlet with a gift in it.
Elizabeth Barrett Browning

GOOD RETURNS

Making a choice about where to contribute financially is something I enjoy doing. I love that money can go places that I cannot go and do things that I cannot do. So when I contribute financially to an organization, I understand that I am supporting its work in the world and so I choose organizations that are engaged in work that uplifts the world. When I think about the work of that organization, if I feel spiritually uplifted and/or fed, then I feel my choice is the correct one. Somehow, somewhere my contribution is making an investment and the return comes in the form of good for people I may never meet.

NOTES

INSPIRATION
FOR TODAY
I have found that among its other benefits, giving liberates the soul of the giver.
Maya Angelou

October 12

GIVE AND IT SHALL
BE GIVEN UNTO YOU

NOTES

Catherine Ponder wrote: "In the past I tithed in a haphazard manner so I received haphazard results. I became bitter and decided tithing was not working for me. I now see it was the manner in which I tithed, and the limited state of my thinking. More recently I have begun to tithe faithfully with love and appreciation for what I have to share."

INSPIRATION
FOR TODAY
*Think of giving not as a
duty but as a privilege.*
John D. Rockerfeller, Jr.

I ATTRACT WHAT I AM

T he Law of Attraction works through you, meaning that you are directly responsible for the quality of your life because you are choosing what to send out. Whether your choices are consciously directed or not, you are automatically attracting into your life exactly what you are sending out.

For some people, hearing this truth is like hearing the morning alarm clock go off at 5:00 a.m. It is a rude awakening. For others, this truth is empowering. Since we are attracting exactly who we are, we can make a conscious choice to change the direction of our thought and create a whole different experience of life.

Dr. Ernest Holmes wrote, "Change your thinking, change your life." Ghandi said, "Be the change you want to see in the world." Become the very person you want to attract. Embody ideas that create health, wealth and success and you will become the very thing you seek.

NOTES _____

_____

_____

_____

INSPIRATION
FOR TODAY
If you keep giving what you're giving, you will keep getting what you're getting.
Chris Michaels

_____

_____

_____

_____

I RECEIVE WHAT I GIVE

NOTES

Life works this way: You can only receive what you are first willing to give.

Emerson wrote, "If you want a friend, be a friend." He understood the way life works. If we want to attract loving people into our lives, we can't hold on to old resentments, hurts and unforgiving thoughts. We get ready to love again by clearing our own hearts of the pain of the past so we can give love freely to another. When we do this, we create a "mental atmosphere" of love around ourselves that automatically attracts people who have the capacity to love us in return.

Before you decide what you want to get from life, take an inventory of what you have to give.

INSPIRATION
FOR TODAY
No one has a right to consume happiness without producing it.
Helen Keller

GRACEFUL GIVING

It is a futile and frustrating effort to keep track of what you give to each person. Rarely does life return our good from the same source to which we gave it. In other words, the people you give the most to are, more than likely, the people you get the least from. Fortunately, others take their place in our lives and end up giving to us, when we have given so little to them.

Giving gracefully means not keeping a record of what you have given to each person. It means giving without thought of what, or when you will receive. Graceful giving is done without ego attachment, so it is not interested in getting credit.

NOTES _____

_____

_____

_____

_____

_____

INSPIRATION
FOR TODAY
*For it is in the giving
that we receive.*
St Francis of Assisi

_____

_____

_____

_____

_____

_____

_____

_____

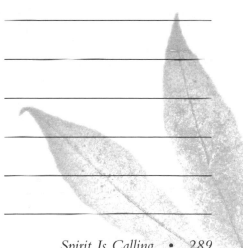

October 16

GRACEFUL RECEIVING

NOTES _____

_____

_____

_____

_____

_____

_____

_____

_____

_____

_____

_____

_____

_____

Never, ever, ever refuse your good! From whatever or whomever it comes, always accept it. If someone gives you a compliment, accept it by saying, "Thank you." If someone wants to give you an expensive gift, take it. If someone offers to pay your way on a trip, accept it. It is *always* appropriate to accept your good in any shape, form or package.

INSPIRATION
FOR TODAY
If someone stops you on the street and invites you to a fine restaurant—go. Let your money come from any direction. If someone says to you, "I want to give you something," and it is at all usable, take it. If it isn't usable, take it anyway and give it to someone else.
Raymond Charles
Barker

If someone gives you something you don't like, take it anyway—and then give it away to someone who will love having it. Keep the circulation of good going.

IT'S OKAY TO ASK

Wisdom begins by questioning. Galileo questioned the official church doctrine which said the sun circles around the earth. Newton asked why the apple fell to the ground. Columbus doubted that the earth was flat. Wondering, asking, and doubting lead to knowing.

Small-minded people believe they have all of the answers. The truly wise know how little they really know.

Never be afraid to ask. There are no stupid questions. There are only questions that remain unasked and knowledge that can't be revealed until they are.

NOTES _____

_____

_____

_____

INSPIRATION
FOR TODAY
He who is afraid of asking
is ashamed of learning.
Danish proverb

_____

_____

_____

_____

_____

_____

_____

_____

_____

_____

October 18
TIME, TALENT, TREASURE

NOTES

You have been given a talent, a unique gift, by your Creator. It is the key to your prosperity. Find out what you can do that no one else can do just like you. And then spend all of your time doing it.

Never work for money. You will never live prosperously if you work for money. Always work for love and joy. Find something you believe in passionately and give all of your time and talent to it. That will make you rich.

INSPIRATION
FOR TODAY
Life is constantly providing us with new funds, new resources, even when we are reduced to immobility. In life's ledger there is no such thing as frozen assets.
Henry Miller

SPIRITUAL LAWS
OF GIVING

The world is full of people who don't understand the basic spiritual laws that govern life. They are trying to get something good to come to them that they're not willing to give to others. They're trying to attract love, without being loving. They're trying to become prosperous, without being generous. They're trying to be happy, without being forgiving.

Here is how Life works:

You can only attract what you are.

You can only receive what you are first willing to give.

Whatever you give to others will return to you.

NOTES

INSPIRATION
FOR TODAY
When we cooperate with spiritual Law and learn how to think, we automatically become powerful and prosperous.
Chris Michaels

October 20
THE FIRST STEP

When I started giving, I began with an amount that I could truly and joyfully set free and then built upon that practice. The result has been that over time, I developed a habit of giving I can feel good about, starting from that beginning point of giving just a little, and over time working up to a substantial amount. This process has helped me carefully examine the atmosphere in which I was giving and it has guided me to clarity about my intentions. I have discovered there is a difference between giving for the joy of giving, and giving with a hidden motive to control or influence. When I notice in my thought that I want anything at all in return for a gift, I call that a deal, or trade.

INSPIRATION
FOR TODAY
*Many people despise
wealth, but few know how
to give it away.*
Francois De La
Rochefoucauld

Giving that is free from expectations of thank you's, recognition, and appreciation opens up a flow of receiving that has no obligations attached. When I give freely, that is when I feel most prosperous.

I DON'T NEED TO KNOW THE OUTCOME

Have you ever received a gift that had strings attached? Sometimes the strings are subtle and might even seem socially acceptable. For example, somebody gives you a watch and checks every time you meet to see if you're wearing it. Or maybe you're someone who gives like that. It could be simply that you want to enjoy the pleasure of seeing the recipient use your gift. On the other hand, have you ever received a gift that had absolutely no strings attached to it whatsoever? For example, somebody gives you a watch and lets you know that you're free to do with it whatever you wish. Or maybe you're someone who gives like that. It may be that you discovered that the joy is in the giving and that in fact you have absolutely no control over how it will be received and used anyway.

What are your thoughts about giving?

NOTES

INSPIRATION
FOR TODAY

Money is like manure; it's not worth a thing unless it's spread around encouraging young things to grow.
Thornton Wilder
The Matchmaker

October 22

THE POINT OF NO RETURN

NOTES

A jet on a runway accelerates until it achieves sufficient speed to be able to take off. At some point, the pilot is committed to the takeoff by having reached a certain momentum, and used up enough runway, that there is no turning back. It's the point of no return. Similarly, committing to someone in a relationship requires going forward without all the information. We have to move into and beyond the point of no return, accepting that there are unknown elements.

Developing a relationship with giving is similar. You can't discover and experience the heart-expanding benefits of giving until you step into and beyond the point of no return. It doesn't matter how many people tell you how wonderful it is; only you can experience it firsthand.

INSPIRATION
FOR TODAY
He that hath a wife and children hath given hostages to fortune.
Francis Bacon

COMMITMENT ACTIVATES ENERGY

W. H. Murray in *The Scottish Himalaya Expedition, 1951,* is said to have written these words: "Until one is committed, there is hesitancy, the chance to draw back, always ineffectiveness. Concerning all acts of initiative (and creation), there is one elementary truth the ignorance of which kills countless ideas and splendid plans: that the moment one definitely commits oneself, the providence moves too. A whole stream of events issues from the decision, raising in one's favor all manner of unforeseen incidents, meetings and material assistance, which no man could have dreamt would have come his way. I learned a deep respect for one of Goethe's couplets: 'Whatever you can do or dream you can, begin it./Boldness has genius, power and magic in it!'"

To me it is a reminder that the real magic is in the moment when we make a commitment. And it is in that moment that energy is activated and we become part of a force that is larger than our commitment. It is as if we unlock the hidden potential of creation, which allows us to accomplish more than we could have ever imagined before the moment of starting.

INSPIRATION
FOR TODAY
What we call the secret of happiness is no more secret than a willingness to choose life.
Leo Buscaglia

NOTES

October 24
I AM NOT AFRAID

NOTES _____

_____

_____

_____

_____

_____

_____

_____

_____

_____

_____

_____

_____

_____

Courage is the ability to continue functioning in the presence of fear, challenges, and the unknown, while continuing to affirm inwardly that the universe with all its mysteries is nevertheless a marvelous place to be. Courage is the willingness to keep on going, to keep on participating, to keep on giving of yourself, while at the same time inwardly affirming that everything is meaningful even if not immediately apparent.

What is the alternative?

INSPIRATION
FOR TODAY
The important thing is this: to be able at any moment to sacrifice what we are for what we would become.
Charles Dubois

LIVING IN THE UNKNOWN

R obert Frost said, "The best way out is always through." And Robert Ingersoll said, "Courage without conscience is a wild beast." These words remind me of the vast unknown in which we live every moment. They remind me that being cautious and careful has its place when doing something delicate, and they also remind me that there are times I let the unknown stop me in my tracks. It is precisely those times when it is necessary for me to look fear in the face and do what is good for me to do.

What is there for you to do today?

NOTES

INSPIRATION FOR TODAY

You gain strength, courage, and confidence by every experience in which you really stop to look fear in the face. You must do the thing which you think you cannot do.
Eleanor Roosevelt

October 26
COMMITTED TO LIVING PROSPEROUSLY

How do you know if you're committed to living prosperously? First of all you have to know what prosperity means to you, and only you can define what prosperity is for you! No one else should be allowed to decide that for you. Advertisers and prosperity teachers have their own ideas about what prosperity is, but what is yours?

INSPIRATION
FOR TODAY
Prosperity is a way of living and thinking, and not just money or things. Poverty is a way of living and thinking, and not just a lack of money or things.
Eric Butterworth

There are very wealthy people who feel poor, and very poor people who feel prosperous. There are people living at every level of income and each tells their own story of what abundance means to them.

Perhaps in the end it's not about money. Could it be about freedom and love?

CONSCIOUS CREATOR

In every person's life a point of awakening occurs. Something happens to wake us up and cause us to realize there is more going on in life than just what meets the eye. It is the soul's appointment with destiny.

As we awaken, we realize there is quite a mess to clean up in our own lives. As we focus on healing our relationships and creating greater peace in our lives, we have a second awakening. We become conscious of the need to contribute something greater to the world than just being one person who healed their past, found love and got rich.

This second awakening is the soul's recognition that we are all *one*. When this happens, you have become a "conscious co-creator," opening your life to a whole new destiny and purpose.

NOTES

INSPIRATION
FOR TODAY

Everything you do counts forever. You are an expression of the whole process of creation; you are a cocreator.
Barbara Marx Hubbard

WHAT AM I CREATING?

Every day is an opportunity to create something new. You do not have to repeat yesterday's experience. You can change. You can do things differently. You can think new thoughts and plan new events.

You are the master of your own fate because you are the only thinker in your mind. You don't have to react negatively to life's challenges. You can respond in a positive way.

INSPIRATION
FOR TODAY
Life isn't about finding yourself. Life is about creating yourself.
George Bernard Shaw

Make of list of ten things you want to create in your life. Use your spiritual practice and prayer to keep them in your conscious awareness until they come to fruition.

IT'S ALWAYS SOMETHING

Your thought is creative, so what you think about, comes about. If you believe that one bad thing happens after another, that's exactly the way life will show up for you. But, if you believe that every day is a new opportunity to succeed, filled with unimaginable blessings, your life will reflect that belief. Events on the outside of your life reflect what's going on inside your mind. Your thought becomes a self-fulfilling prophecy.

Successful people think about success. What are *you* thinking about?

NOTES

INSPIRATION
FOR TODAY

When we think of failure; Failure will be ours. If we remain undecided; Nothing will ever change. All we need to do is want to achieve something great and then simply to do it. Never think of failure For what we think, will come about.
Maharishi Mahesh Yogi

October 30
FREE TO EXPRESS

Pretentious people are pretending to be something they're not, because they don't believe that what they are is good enough. So, they try to imitate others who they hold in higher regard than themselves. This always fails in the end because you can only go on pretending for so long. Inevitably the real you will always come out.

INSPIRATION
FOR TODAY
I stand for freedom of expression, doing what you believe in, and going after your dreams.
Madonna

Why not let it out today? What do you fear? Are you afraid of what others might think or how they may respond? What control do you have over their thoughts anyway?

Be yourself. Don't waste your time on cheap imitations. Follow the dream in your own heart all the way to the destiny your Creator intended. Let loose on the world your authentic self.

AN OUTLET FOR SPIRIT

Your spirit, soul and body have been created by Life as an outlet for God. Life gave you your talent. It beats your heart. It sustains your life. It is the wisdom that guides you and the heart inside that allows you to love and be loved in return. Without God, you have no existence.

Your life is a once-in-a-lifetime opportunity for God to experience and express itself as *you*. Seek conscious union with your Creator. Ask to know its Presence and feel its Perfect Love. Call on its Wisdom to flow through your mind unobstructed.

NOTES

INSPIRATION
FOR TODAY
I am a red man. If the Great Spirit had desired me to be a white man he would have made me so in the first place.
Sitting Bull

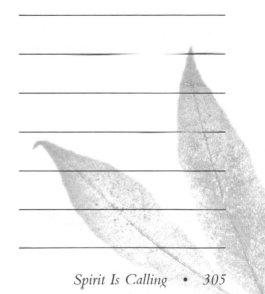

THE MIND OF GOD

Imagine the depth of a mind that can conceive a universe. Imagine the possibilities that it can conceive. Knowing no limits to its own power and authority, the mind of God is not limited to time and space. It knows no sequence. It has no awareness of hard or easy, big or small.

It thinks through its creation—through you. It pours its new ideas into your mind every day. It gives itself freely, without obligation or expectation.

INSPIRATION FOR TODAY

All invention, art, literature, government, law and wisdom that has come to the race has been given to it through those who have deeply penetrated the secrets of nature and the mind of God.

Dr. Ernest Holmes

The key to your success can be found in what new ideas are rising to be known in your mind. They are God's gift to you, given freely, with the intention of prospering your life. Don't abort those Divine ideas with fear and doubt. Have faith in them. They will guide you to the next step on your path.

I AM CREATIVE

Beethoven had a flash of inspiration that came to him in one great chord. In the time it took to snap his finger, he heard an entire symphony. It took him weeks to write it down and it takes an entire hour for an orchestra to play it. Beethoven's short burst of Divine inspiration brought music to the world that is still being played centuries later.

Sometimes what our Creator can reveal in just a moment takes us ten years to find the courage to do something about. But if we open our minds, we will hear the voice of Spirit eager to give us the very thing we need to fulfill ourselves.

NOTES

INSPIRATION
FOR TODAY
If one advances confidently in the direction of his dreams, and endeavors to live the life which he has imagined, he will meet with a success unexpected in common hours.
Henry David Thoreau

November 3

I AM AN ORIGINAL

I once pulled on a loose thread in a hand knitted sweater. It didn't seem important. It was tucked away in a seam. I was certain that my sweater would be fine, even better without this spot of untidiness.

I was wrong. What I set in motion by pulling that thread was the eventual undoing of my favorite sweater. I didn't notice it at first, but in time the unraveling was quite serious. Apparently my sweater, without that thread, was not complete, and couldn't hold itself together, and would eventually collapse.

INSPIRATION
FOR TODAY
No matter what age you are, or what your circumstances might be, you are special, and you still have something unique to offer. Your life, because of who you are, has meaning.
Barbara de Angelis

Maybe you fit into life in the same way. Even when you're untidy or feeling over-looked. What would unravel without you?

I TRUST MY CREATIVITY

Betty Edwards writes, "Most children between the ages of about nine and eleven have a passion for realistic drawing. They become sharply critical of their childhood drawings and begin to draw certain favorite subjects over and over again, attempting to perfect the image. Anything short of perfect realism may be regarded as failure."

Whether from their own observation or from the adults around them, some children learn to abandon their creativity as a result of this too-perfect standard. It can be carried over into almost anything in life. Where are you trapped by an all too severe standard of perfection?

NOTES

INSPIRATION
FOR TODAY
When you realize how perfect everything is you will tilt your head back and laugh at the sky.
Gautama Siddharta
Buddha

November 5
CONNECTED TO CREATION

NOTES

"In the beginning" is a phrase frequently used to begin a creation story. Everything starts in the beginning, and before the beginning there wasn't a thing. So I imagine that everything in creation is made out of the same building blocks...Creation itself. Imagine that. you are made out of the only thing Creation had available in the beginning...Itself.

INSPIRATION
FOR TODAY
I am as my creator made me and since He is satisfied, so am I.
Minnie Smith

WHAT I THINK MATTERS

It may seem to some people that their thoughts are private and separate from the world, and therefore what they think does not matter to anyone but themselves. Even if this were true — which it's not—the content of their thoughts certainly matters to their own experience of the world around them. Take for example a person whose thought is "I am capable" and imagine the impact of that thought on the way the person conducts himself. Compare that to the conduct of a person whose thought is "I am incapable."

Step one in activating creativity in your life is noticing what thought happens in your mind and then noticing how that matters to you. Today, notice the effect it has on how you treat people, yourself and your world. By the end of today, it is possible that you might have greater insight into why some people say "thought is creative."

NOTES

INSPIRATION
FOR TODAY
*What we think,
we become.*
Gautama
Siddhartha Buddha

November 7

WHAT I SAY MATTERS

NOTES

_____

_____

_____

_____

_____

_____

_____

_____

_____

_____

_____

_____

_____

_____

INSPIRATION
FOR TODAY
*Speech is the mirror
of the soul; as a man
speaks, so he is.*
Publilius Syrus

Some wise person said that what comes out of the mouth is more important than what goes into it. What we say and how we say it gives people around us a valuable insight into what we believe and value. Even when saying something we don't mean, or something frivolous, our words paint a picture in which our character can actually be seen. Here is a wonderful experiment. Give yourself 24 wordless hours. It is possible that by the end of such a day without speaking, you will have an awareness into why some people believe that words are powerful.

WHAT I DO MATTERS

By their deeds they shall be known. This saying of Jesus points out the importance of action when it comes to activating creativity in life. A thoughtful meditation may yield inspiration and a beautiful concept. It may also help to tell a friend or mentor about the idea received to consolidate the vision. But nothing happens until something is done. What you do, matters.

NOTES

INSPIRATION
FOR TODAY
*Inaction may be the
biggest form of action.*
Jerry Brown

AUTHENTIC LIVING

Live your own authentic life so that when it is time to move on, you can feel confident that you were yourself and not someone else. Or worse, imagine discovering that you spent your life trying to be someone or something that other people wanted you to be.

The mirror image of this idea of being your authentic self is letting other people live authentically too by removing any demands you might have for how they should be or what they should do, or who they should love or what they should accomplish.

INSPIRATION FOR TODAY

One of the characteristics of great drawings is the artist's wholehearted acceptance of his own style and character. It is as if the drawing says for the artist, "Here I am."
Nathan Goldstein

A LIFE IN PROGRESS

O ur paths are revealed only one step at a time. We don't know what tomorrow may bring—and that's a good thing.

Though it may appear that you are wandering from one thing to the next, from the proper distance it can be seen that you were always on the right path. You have never been lost. You have been exploring!

NOTES _____

_____

_____

_____

_____

INSPIRATION
FOR TODAY

I don't need to completely understand the big picture to know that my role is important. I don't have to know the destination to know I'm headed in the right direction. Though I may not know where I am going, I'm not lost, I am exploring.
Jana Stanfield

_____

_____

_____

_____

_____

_____

_____

ENJOY THE PROCESS

In school, when the teacher asks a question, the person who has the correct answer raises their hand first. Life is not like that. It's not about finding the answers first. The person who rushes through life unconsciously gets to the end of it with a lot of regrets. You've heard it said a thousand times, but it's still true: Life is a journey, not a destination!

INSPIRATION
FOR TODAY
*This life is a process
of learning.*
Lauryn Hill

Stop and look around. Maybe there's something nearby that's worth looking at. Perhaps the answers to the questions you've had for so long are right in front of your eyes.

Have fun. Don't take life so seriously. It's not a joke—but it's also not a job. Explore a little. See your life as an adventure story instead of a life sentence. Enjoy the process.

THE JOY OF PARTICIPATION

When you do what brings you the most joy, it's easy to lose track of time. An hour seems to pass like a minute. If your birthdays come as a huge surprise to you each year, it's probably because you are living a joyful life.

Keep your center of joy. Guard it. Don't allow the drudgery of day-to-day living to infect your joy. Keep dancing through life joyfully!

NOTES _____

_____

_____

_____

_____

INSPIRATION
FOR TODAY
While I dance I cannot judge, I cannot hate, I cannot separate myself from life. I can only be joyful and whole. That is why I dance.
Hans Bos

_____

_____

_____

_____

_____

_____

_____

_____

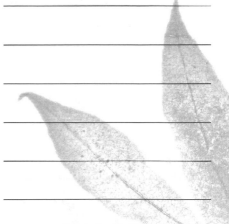

November 13
CREATION FROM CHAOS

NOTES

If you watch the news and view the world too closely, it appears that everything is in chaos. But if you view our world from space, you can't see the boundaries of nations or the crime in the streets. All that is visible is a peaceful blue globe floating beautifully in space.

This same truth applies to your life. Don't look too closely or judge too quickly. Out of chaos comes creativity. And just below the surface of what appears to be chaos is complete order.

INSPIRATION
FOR TODAY
Our real discoveries come from chaos, from going to the place that looks wrong and stupid and foolish.
Chuck Palahniuk

Try something new today. Go somewhere you've never been. Talk to somebody you've never spoken to before.

JUDGE NOT BY APPEARANCE

Things are not as they appear. We are not the bodies that reflect an image in the mirror. We are spirits encased in these bodies.

Our value doesn't come from our education or assets. It comes from our connection to God. No one is "better" because they live in an expensive house or drive a luxury car. We all hold equal value in the eyes of God.

Try to see beyond appearances. Don't be fooled by the way things look. We are more than we appear to be. Pierce the thin veneer of what appears to be real and you will see the Truth about these souls that occupy Earth. We are angels in disguise!

NOTES

INSPIRATION FOR TODAY

Judgments prevent us from seeing the good that lies beyond appearances.
Wayne Dyer

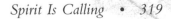

November 15

A JOURNEY, NOT A DESTINATION

In his autobiograpy, Nikos Kazantzakis, author of *Zorba the Greek*, described an incident in which he came upon a cocoon in the woods just as the butterfly was making a hole, trying to emerge. Impatient for results, he bent over and warmed it with his breath to speed up the process. The butterfly, however, emerged prematurely with its wings hopelessly crumbled. It needed the sun's slow warmth to give it time to build the energy necessary for flight. Moments later, after a desperate struggle, the butterfly died in the palm of his hand.

INSPIRATION
FOR TODAY
The journey is the reward.
Chinese proverb

The message of this unfortunate saga is that nature has its own time and place for our good to emerge. It cannot be forced or scheduled for our convenience.

Do you remember a time in your life when you tried to force something to happen that wasn't ready to happen? What were the results?

THE CREATIVE PROCESS

God is not cruel. It did not create your life as an experience to suffer through. Nor was life designed as an obstacle course for you to fight your way through.

God creates out of a desire for Self-expression, just as any great artist would do. It creates manifestations of perfect ideas. It's only purpose is to express beauty, love and joy.

Your life is supposed to be a joyful experience. You are not here to work hard, climb the corporate ladder and compete for your good. You are here to express yourself fully and live joyfully.

Remember this:

You are not here to learn, you are here to *live*.

You are not here to get the best, you are here to *give* the best.

You are not here to win, you are here to have a *spiritual experience*.

NOTES

INSPIRATION
FOR TODAY
*Many people feel that God
intended them to have a
life of suffering and
hardship, and is it any
wonder that that is what
they have?*
Dr. Ernest Holmes

November 17
WITHOUT DELAYS

The moment you're living in is the only moment where you exist. You may have heard this idea expressed in endless ways by spiritual teachers and self-help methods. It bears repeating because not only is it reality, it is also one of those ideas that is so simple it can easily be overlooked. One of the ways I avoid being in the present moment is to put things off that I fear doing now. Sometimes this is a good choice, giving me time to gather my wits and calm my nerves. Other times, I use delay as a way of avoiding what is in front of me to do.

INSPIRATION
FOR TODAY
*You may delay,
but time will not.*
Benjamin Franklin

I've made a list of all the things I've put off doing now, whether it's because I don't have the time, or I don't want to, or I'm afraid to. After making the list, I notice that there are a number of items on the list that I don't really have to do. Some of them I placed on the list out of a sense of obligation. Others I can't even remember why it seemed that someday I should do them.

What's on your list of delayed items?

322 • *Spirit Is Calling*

I BRING FORTH
WHAT IS WITHIN ME

Creation surrounds us with its intelligence and energy. That same intelligence and energy is in us and can be accessed to find direction and patterns of meaning. You can practice bringing forth the creative genius within you by stimulating your mind to address problems and situations in new and novel ways. For example, by asking yourself questions about a difficult situation, or about a decision you have to make, can help bring forth a wealth of wisdom from within you. Ask questions such as, "How does someone from another culture view this situation?" Or, "Is there some way in which I could flourish even though this is going on?"

What examples of creative questions can you think of that would help the innate wisdom in you come forth today?

NOTES

INSPIRATION
FOR TODAY
*The Lord whose oracle
is at Delphi neither
indicates clearly nor
conceals but gives a sign.*
Heraclitus

A DREAM DEFERRED

Langston Hughes's famous poem, "A Dream Deferred," asks the reader to consider the downside of not living our dreams. He was one of the most important writers and thinkers of the Harlem Renaissance, the African-American artistic movement in the 1920s that celebrated black life and culture. Through his work, which included children's books, poetry, plays and more, he spoke for equality and justice and contributed significantly to American literature and politics.

Imagine if he postponed bringing forth what was in him?

What is yours to do today?

INSPIRATION
FOR TODAY
Hold fast to dreams for if dreams die, life is a broken winged bird that cannot fly.
Langston Hughes

ILLUSIONS

There is no question that people are creative. Creativity is required every single moment in the maintenance of personal reality. The world as it appears around us is perceived through our sensory organs and reported to our mind where we constantly interpret and create meaning, connections and so much more. This is exactly how personal reality is born. It is an invention of your personal creativity.

What does "I am not cre-ative" mean?

NOTES

INSPIRATION FOR TODAY
The task of the real intellectual consists of analyzing illusions in order to discover their causes.
Arthur Miller

November 21

OPPORTUNITIES

NOTES

Life seldom shows up with clearly defined margins or boundaries. We have to put our own patterns of order on the world to make sense of it. We use ideas and language, art and culture to organize life.

This is fantastic! It suggests that everything is an opportunity to be re-expressed and re-organized in thought and understanding. For example, where does your hand end and your arm begin? Practicing this kind of reframing is activating spirituality in your life, and it is one of the most important keys to spiritual progress: the ability to be flexible in understanding and defining the world around you.

Pick some situation you are dealing with and try to describe it using completely different words than you would usually choose. You might want to get your Thesaurus for this exercise and look up synonyms for the definitions you have placed on life.

INSPIRATION
FOR TODAY
Every creative act involves…a new innocence of perception, liberated from the cataract of accepted belief.
Arthur Koestler

BREAKING
THROUGH BARRIERS

A helpful technique for breaking through moments of being stuck in thinking is to actively consider the opposite point of view in a certain way. Take for example a disagreement with a colleague or friend. Write down what they have expressed that you do not agree with. Now, try to think of at least three ways in which their statement is actually true.

Have fun.

NOTES

INSPIRATION
FOR TODAY
One of life's most fulfilling moments occurs in that split second when the familiar is suddenly transformed into the dazzling aura of the profoundly new...
Edward B. Lindaman

November 23

THERE ARE NO BLOCKS

Probably the most challenging blocks of all to discover and face are those within our own thoughts. Recognizing how we place obstacles in our way, sometimes without even being aware that we are doing so, takes courage and determination. However, once you start this kind of inquiry, you get better and better at noticing what is really a thing to go around and what is something to go through.

INSPIRATION
FOR TODAY
There is nothing more real than nothing.
Samuel Beckett

Maybe the thing to do is to seek out the boundaries we have placed around our lives. Do they relate to energy, happiness, creativity, relationship? Maybe the thing to do is to find out what patterns of thought we have that feel like blocks to progress and then practice thinking something else. This is all about activating creativity in your life, so why not try it? What is there to lose?

CYCLES AND RHYTHMS

The circle is our oldest symbol for God—-it represents the never-ending cycle of life.

The universe has a pulse or rhythm. It is a living organism filled with the Presence of Life (God). Everything in nature moves in cycles. This is also true of your life, because you are connected to all life in the universe.

Because this is so, change is inevitable. Things are not supposed to stay the same.

You have a choice: You can go with the flow of life and see change as good, or you can try to resist it. Either way, things will change. The only difference is what *your* life will look like in the midst of it.

NOTES

INSPIRATION
FOR TODAY
*That which the fountain
sends forth returns again to
the fountain.*
Henry Wadsworth
Longfellow

November 25
TIME OUT

Take time today to do nothing!

INSPIRATION
FOR TODAY
*Rest is not idleness, and to
lie sometimes on the grass
under the trees on a sum-
mer's day, listening to the
murmur of water, or watching the clouds float across
the sky, is by no means a
waste of time.*
John Lubbock

REFUELING WITHIN

You already know the answers to the questions you keep asking others. You know exactly what to do.

We don't get into trouble because we don't know what to do. We get into trouble because we don't do what we know we should have done all along.

Inside you is a place of wisdom and peace. Go there often and reawaken your spirit.

NOTES

_____

_____

_____

_____

_____

INSPIRATION
FOR TODAY
*Your vision will become
clear only when you look
into your heart. Who looks
outside, dreams. Who looks
inside, awakens.*
Carl Jung

_____

_____

_____

_____

_____

_____

_____

November 27
REST

Take time to rest today and listen to music that lifts your spirit and heals your soul!

INSPIRATION
FOR TODAY
Music speaks what cannot be expressed, soothes the mind and gives it rest, heals the heart and makes it whole, flows from heaven to the soul.
Unknown

RECREATE

Go to a museum or art gallery and find an artist who inspires you. Sit in front of the artwork and contemplate yourself and your life choices. Think of what you want to recreate. How do you want to reinvent yourself?

NOTES _____

_____

_____

_____

_____

INSPIRATION
FOR TODAY
*The effort of art is
to keep what is interesting
in existence, to recreate it
in the eternal.*
George Santayana

_____

_____

_____

_____

_____

_____

_____

_____

_____

November 29
NO ACTIVITY

NOTES

T ake a moment today to stop *all* activity and stimulation. No TV, radio or external noise. Sit in the silence and wait until you hear the voice of God.

What is it saying to you?

INSPIRATION
FOR TODAY
How beautiful it is to do nothing, and then rest afterward.
Spanish proverb

PRACTICING THE SABBATH

E very day is holy. Every place is sacred.

Take one day a week to address your spiritual needs. Go somewhere inspiring. Remind yourself that life is about something greater than just work and paying bills. Revisit your spirit.

On the Sabbath, gather around you the people you love. Spend time together talking, listening and laughing. Enjoy the life you've created for yourself and be thankful for the many blessings that you have received.

NOTES

INSPIRATION
FOR TODAY
*God blessed the seventh
day and made it holy,
because on that day
he rested…*
Genesis 2:3

December 1
JOYFUL LIVING

NOTES

The words "happiness" and "joy" are defined in similar ways. I tend to think of happiness as attached to something: a gift, an outcome, a result, an accomplishment. Joy, on the other hand, has no cause. It does not depend on anything at all. It is not generated or increased or diminished. It is the foundation of life. Happiness has the disadvantage of being transitory and dependent. Oh, I have nothing against happiness, but I do love joy.

How do you define happiness and joy?

INSPIRATION
FOR TODAY
I think of Joy as permanent, and happiness as conditional.
Edward Viljoen

JOY AND LAUGHTER

J oy has may forms, from quiet and soulful (as in watching a sunset) to energetic and uplifting (as in seeing an old friend again after a long absence). Joy has many other forms, too. One form is connected to laughter. It is different for every person…and whatever it is that gives you deep satisfying laugher is a clue to where your center of joy is.

What makes you laugh?

NOTES _____

_____

_____

_____

_____

_____

_____

_____

_____

_____

_____

_____

_____

INSPIRATION
FOR TODAY
*Laughter is the shortest
distance between
two people.*
Victor Borge

December 3
KEEPING JOY ALIVE

NOTES

Perhaps the first step in keeping joy alive is to acknowledge that Joy can never die. There are times when Joy seems to be absent or distant, but there are very specific things that you can do to bring it closer. For example, initiating a change of pace and surroundings can be very helpful to bring joy into a fuller flow. If you've been spending a lot of time around people, the change might be to spend some time alone. If you've been isolated and working intensely, the change might be to go visiting or do something in nature. Another exercise is to make a list of the things you used to do in your childhood that gave you joy. Even if those things are as simplistic as coloring or daydreaming, set aside a special day for yourself to do one or two of those things.

Joy is at home and particularly alive when innocence is present.

INSPIRATION
FOR TODAY
The Constitution only guarantees the American people the right to pursue happiness. You have to catch it yourself.
Benjamin Franklin

MY RIGHT TO BE HAPPY

You have a right to be happy! Well, on closer examination that statement might more accurately be expressed as, "You have a right to be what you are." Or better still, "You are what you are, and that's alright." Probably, you have the right to be any way you want to be. When I first heard that idea, it was news to me. It opened up a world of possibility for me. To test whether or not happiness is something available regardless of what is going on around me has been my ongoing quest since encountering the idea. Sometimes I'm more successful than others. I'm most successful when I don't try to force anything, especially not a cheerful, make-believe-everything-is-ok-when-it-is-not approach to life. It's given me many opportunities to look into happiness and what I think it is and what I think causes it.

What brings you happiness and why? Make a list of the things and people you love, including everything and everyone: family, friends, music, books, ideas, places, pets, etc.

NOTES

INSPIRATION FOR TODAY
You and I are born out of God, and we are born out of a divine urge that creates.
Ernest Holmes

December 5
HAVING FUN

What do you do for fun? What are the activities that bring you pleasure? What is it about them that makes them so enjoyable? How do you feel about yourself when you're engaged in them?

Some people feel the pressure of culture and do not let themselves have as much fun as they want to. They impose boundaries on what they allow themselves to do. Some of these restrictions have a useful role in maintaining balance, but some restrictions have to go! What limits do you place on yourself that need to go?

When last did you have fun and what were you doing?

INSPIRATION
FOR TODAY
*We have a song to sing;
we have a joy to bring
to the world.*
Ernest Holmes

BEING SILLY

A teacher once counseled me to take a serious look at nature to discover all the silliness that Creation had indulged. I had never thought of life in quite that way. However, after a day of noticing the most bizarre insects, outrageous plants, pointless patterns, overindulgences, lavish displays, I got it. Creation is utterly and completely out there! There seems to be a forward rush of creativity that is sometimes ecstatic, sometimes hilarious, sometimes sublime.

All of this is in you. All of it.

When last were you silly and what were you doing?

NOTES

INSPIRATION
FOR TODAY
We are born to create, and we can't help it. Why is that? Because God, the great Creator, is in us.
Ernest Holmes

December 7
HAPPINESS AND JOY

NOTES
NOTES _____

_____

_____

_____

_____

_____

_____

_____

_____

_____

_____

_____

_____

_____

_____

O ne of the happiest days of my life was spent one summer, white-water rafting with a group of friends. We had a blast! That day is deeply embedded in my memory.

Think back to one of the happiest days of your life. What were the surroundings? What were you doing? Who was there with you?

What can you do to create more days like that?

INSPIRATION
FOR TODAY
If you want to be happy, be.
Leo Tolstoy

STRESS-FREE LIVING

Stress is not a disease. It is manufactured in the minds of men and women. It is a negative reaction to life, a self-induced sense of being over-whelmed. And yet it has a profound effect on our lives. Stress is the number one contributor to heart disease and a host of other physical problems.

Living a stress-free life means taking time out of every day to restore and regenerate your soul. Meditation and prayer are great tools to relieve stress. Taking frequent breaks and vacations are also helpful. Taking care of yourself is a sign of healthy self-esteem.

What can you do to reduce your stress level?

NOTES

INSPIRATION
FOR TODAY
Stress is nothing more than a socially acceptable form of mental illness.
Richard Carlson

December 9
LASTING JOY

NOTES

No one can make you happy. Happiness is a choice you make every-day. No one can make you miser-able. Misery is a choice you make everyday. Which will you choose today?

INSPIRATION
FOR TODAY

The great teachings unani-mously emphasize that all the peace, wisdom, and joy in the universe are already within us; we don't have to gain, develop, or attain them. We're like a child standing in a beautiful park with his eyes shut tight. We don't need to imagine trees, flowers, deer, birds, and sky; we merely need to open our eyes and realize what is already here, who we really are—as soon as we quit pretending we're small or unholy.
Unknown

THE PURSUIT OF HAPPINESS

Happiness can't be chased or hunted down. It's not something you find somewhere. It doesn't come from other people, or from owning more stuff, or having lots of money. Happiness is something you *are*. It's in your nature to be happy. It's natural and normal.

Being happy is easy. All you have to do is spend time doing things that bring you joy. Spend time with people who make you laugh. Do work that you enjoy.

Give up the idea that there is any virtue in suffering or being unhappy. God is Joy!

NOTES

INSPIRATION
FOR TODAY
*Happiness comes of
the capacity to feel deeply,
to enjoy simply, to think
freely, to risk life,
to be needed.*
Storm Jameson

December 11
STUFF AND THINGS

There used to be a popular bumper sticker that read, "The one with the most toys, wins." Nothing could be further from the truth.

Life is not about acquisition. We're not here to accumulate stuff and things. We're here to have a spiritual experience.

INSPIRATION
FOR TODAY
*The things you own
end up owning you.*
Tyler Durden

When you achieve a true prosperity consciousness, you realize you can have anything you want. When you know you can have anything, ironically, you want very little.

Be more: own less stuff!

THE BEST THINGS IN LIFE...

L ove is free. Wisdom is free. Joy is free. Peace is free. Health is free. Everything of true value has no cost. They are gifts of Spirit, given freely to anyone who is ready to receive.

These are the gifts people need the most. They don't need more stuff; they need more love and attention. They need sound advice from a friend, or someone to laugh with. People need encouragement. They don't need another piece of junk that will eventually end up in a garage sale.

Get off the merry-go-round of materialism and rampant consumerism. Give something people really need. Write a poem to your lover. Tell a friend what you respect and admire about them. Give a co-worker a pat on the back. Encourage someone you know to keep working toward their dreams.

NOTES

INSPIRATION
FOR TODAY
*The best things in life
are free.*
American proverb

December 13

JOY IS MY NATURE

One of the songs people sing during the holidays is, "Joy to the World." But the question is: Who is responsible for bringing joy to the world? You are!

Don't wait for the world to become joyful. Let the joy that lives in your heart come pouring out into the world. Give it to friends, loved ones, family members and strangers. Smile at someone across the room. It doesn't matter whether you know them or not.

Practice expressing joy and watch what happens. You will begin to attract happier people.

INSPIRATION
FOR TODAY
Fill your life with as many moments and experiences of joy and passion as you humanly can.
Marcia Wieder

PROTECTING MY HEART OF JOY

Against whom should you protect your heart of joy? Probably the only person who can steal it! You. And the best line of protection is to develop your character so that you definitely become the kind of person who would never think of stealing your own joy!

The way you do this is by practicing daily to think highly of yourself and then to follow that up with words, actions and habits that reflect this high esteem. Then you can go about supporting this idea with internal dialogue that is consistent with high regard.

The moment we begin to develop a wholesome relationship with ourselves is the moment we begin providing a safe harbor for our heart of joy.

NOTES

INSPIRATION
FOR TODAY
Don't worry, be happy.
Bobby McFerrin

December 15
GIVING JOY

NOTES

Activating joy in your life has so much to do with how you think about and relate to other people. Incorporating genuine affection for others is a powerful way of generating immediate results. The trick to giving joy is simplicity and secrecy. In other words, don't over-do anything and don't make a big fuss about your affection. Don't worry about whether or not it is noticed or acknowl-edged. Do it as if you're on a secret assignment to love.

In a way, this is exactly how Spirit loves us.

INSPIRATION
FOR TODAY
Each needs to express the Life within him in his own way, but never at the expense of another.
Ernest Holmes

IN THE PRESENCES OF JOY

Who in your life do you enjoy spending time with? Who brings you joy just from being in their company? Fortunately, happiness is contagious. Spend time with truly joyful people and you'll catch some, even if it takes a while. It's similar to spending time with people who are all prayed up—their confidence and peace of mind affect us just from being close to them.

What do people experience in your presence?

NOTES

December 17
A RECIPE FOR JOY

NOTES

Imagine you were creating a foolproof recipe for a joyful life. Imagine it would become the guiding principles for a group of young people setting off into the world on their own.

What would your recipe be? What has proven to be indispensable for experiencing joy in your life?

INSPIRATION
FOR TODAY
*Success is not the key
to happiness. Happiness
is the key to success.*
Albert Schweitzer.

AUTHENTIC GIVING

If you've ever been on the receiving end of a gift that was wrapped up with obligation and expectation, you know how that feels. In my opinion, a gift that expects anything in return is not a gift at all. It's more like a business deal. On the other hand, I cherish the moments when I really get it right and give a gift that is so perfectly in tune with the receiver that their face can't help but brighten up. But I have learned over the years that being attached to that outcome is a certain recipe for disaster. Better for me is to give for the simple joy of giving. That's why I spend so much time wrapping presents. I'm not very good at it, but it helps me draw out the authentic experience of being excited about what I'm about to do.

NOTES

INSPIRATION FOR TODAY
If only we'd stop trying to be happy we'd have a pretty good time.
Edith Wharton

December 19
THE LIFE LINE

NOTES

The Life Line to happiness is gratitude. People are often better at counting their troubles than they are at counting their joys. But that is something that can be improved with very little effort. Simply making a list of everything and anything that you feel any kind of gratitude for will get you started.

INSPIRATION
FOR TODAY
*What a wonderful life
I've had. I only wish I'd
realized it sooner.*
Colette

DRAW NEAR

When Winnie the Pooh was about to explain what he liked doing best, he had to stop for a moment and think about it. He was going to say that eating honey was the thing he liked best, but he remembered the moment just before eating honey, and thought that moment to be even better than when you are actually eating the honey.

Some people miss the moments that lead up to their goals and dreams and overlook the treasure of being here and now.

NOTES

**INSPIRATION
FOR TODAY**

*The foolish man seeks
happiness in the distance;
the wise man grows it
under his feet.*
James Openheim

December 21
THE GIFT OF SPIRIT IS JOY

NOTES

It's easy to focus on the happiness that comes from getting a thing. But the joy that comes from seeing and appreciating what we already have is wonderful. Spirit is another word for reality, and reality is what we already have. Seeing and appreciating what we have is a way of taking in the awesome wonder that reality is and discovering the joy that is packed solid into everything.

INSPIRATION
FOR TODAY
Happiness is the soundtrack of my life.
Grey Livingston

LIGHT

L ight was the first creation. It is a metaphor representing the Presence of God. Where there is no light, there is no truth. Where there is no truth, fear grows.

When you are afraid, remember the truth that God is always with you. Every day you live in the Presence of all the power you need to overcome your challenges. You are enveloped in God's grace and love. You are surrounded by its healing Presence.

NOTES

INSPIRATION
FOR TODAY
Fear grows in the darkness;
if you think there's a
bogeyman around,
turn on the light.
Dorothy Thompson

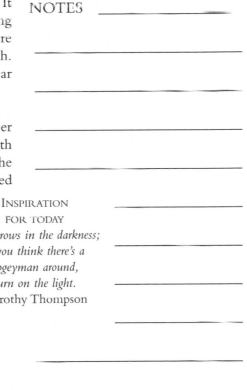

December 23

I AM WITH YOU

NOTES

You are never alone. The Creator of your life is also the Sustainer of your body. It lives in, as and through you. It is the wisdom that moves through your mind and the love that flows out from your heart. God is alive, within and around you!

Take time today to feel its Presence.

INSPIRATION
FOR TODAY
...I have chosen you,
I have not rejected you,
do not be afraid,
for I am with you...
Isaiah 41:10

December 24

EXPECT GOOD

As a strategy for life, a lot of people expect very little, thinking they won't be disappointed if very little shows up. That's not a good strategy, because what you expect shows up in your life. If you expect very little from life, that's exactly what you'll get.

Building your level of expectation so that you wake up each day expecting life to be good is a full-time occupation. It requires your constant attention to avoid going the way of the world and being pulled downward into mediocrity. The world is happy to maintain the status quo, but that is not good enough for you. You deserve better!

NOTES

INSPIRATION
FOR TODAY
*Excellence can be
obtained if you:
...care more than others
think is wise;
...risk more than others
think is safe;
...dream more than others
think is practical;
...expect more than others
think is possible.*
Unknown

December 25

MANY BLESSINGS

Your life is a blessing, even when it seems not to be. You are alive. You have the freedom to make a new choice and effect everything in your life from this day forward. You have the unique gift of your own character and personality. No one is quite like you. There are many things to be grateful for today. Even when things happen that don't appear to be a blessing, oftentimes they turn out to be exactly that.

Don't withhold blessings from others if you don't want them withheld from you. Give your blessings to anyone who has found love or anyone who finds joy in what they do. The blessing you give to others return tenfold to you.

INSPIRATION
FOR TODAY
May your days be many and your troubles be few. May all God's blessings descend upon you. May peace be within you may your heart be strong. May you find what you're seeking wherever you roam.
Irish blessing

If you want to work for peace in the world, start inside your own mind. Clear away the confusion and self-doubt. Rid yourself of the bitterness. Reject the cynic. Expel the monkey chatter that constantly goes back and forth between self-acceptance and self-degradation. Dispose of the inner critic.

Then, work to establish peace in your own heart. Forgive everyone, no matter what they did to hurt you. Forgive your-self for not knowing better and for making poor choices. Let go of every resentment. Cleanse your heart of all jealousy and judgment.

Now you're ready to work for peace in the world.

NOTES

INSPIRATION
FOR TODAY
There can never be peace between nations until there is first known that true peace which is within the souls of men.
Black Elk

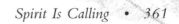

December 27
ALL IS WELL

Most of the pain we carry around with us doesn't come from anything that's happening in the present moment. It is unhealed and unprocessed pain from the past. Since this is the only moment you really have, it makes sense to be fully conscious and present. This will allow you to release the past, forget about the future and experience all that life has put in front of you.

INSPIRATION FOR TODAY
The ability to be in the present moment is a major component of mental wellness.
Abraham Maslow

Like anything else, being present in the moment takes practice. Try this the next time you engage in conversation: Fully listen to what the other person is saying. Be present. Resist thinking about how you feel about what they're saying, or what you want to say next. Just stay present and listen. Stay in the moment.

Very few people have the ability to be fully present. But you can be one of them. With practice, you will be living your life right where it is, not regretting your past or planning your future. The truth is that right now, all is well!

CELEBRATING LIFE

Do you celebrate your successes? Do you take time to make a list of what you've accomplished and applaud yourself?

Many people are so focused on what needs to be done in the future, they forget to celebrate what they've already accomplished. Take a look at what you've done. You'll be amazed at how far you've come in just a year.

Take time today to celebrate who you are. Do something special for yourself to honor your accomplishments.

NOTES

INSPIRATION
FOR TODAY
*Celebrate the happiness
that friends are always
giving, make every day
a holiday and celebrate
just living!*
Amanda Bradley

December 29

LOOKING BACK

The end of the year is near. Much has happened—some of it good, some of it challenging. There are things you are proud of, and things you'd like to forget. But all of it has brought you here, to the person you are right now. Every challenge you faced made you wiser or stronger in some way.

What do you know now that you didn't know at the beginning of the year? What wisdom have you gained?

INSPIRATION
FOR TODAY
*What you need to know about the past is that no matter what has happened, it has all worked together to bring you to this very moment. And this is the moment you can choose to make everything new;
Right now.*
"Touched By An Angel"
CBS

LOOKING INWARD

The key to your success next year is in the ideas that are present in your mind today. Go within and release judgment. Have a creative "jam session," allowing the free flow of new ideas to come pouring out of you, without trying to figure out how they're going to come into fruition. No idea is too silly or unreasonable. Then select from all of them the ones you want to concentrate your energies on.

Knowledge comes from education. It is an external event. Wisdom comes from being present to the Inner Knower within you. Seek first the wisdom within you, and then all else will be added.

NOTES

INSPIRATION
FOR TODAY

Creative ideas reside in people's minds but are trapped by fear or rejection. Create a judgment-free environment and you'll unleash a torrent of creativity.

Alex Osborne

December 31
LOOKING FORWARD

NOTES _____

The year is over. Count your blessings. Take the wisdom you have gained and go forward. Make a new plan. Follow your best ideas. Dream new dreams. You are the captain of your own ship. You can set sail to wherever you want to go.

Nothing can stop you now! You are starting out on a grand, new adventure. You are guided by wisdom, surrounded by love and propelled by God's powerful force.

INSPIRATION
FOR TODAY
Count your blessings.
Once you realize how
valuable you are and how
much you have going for
you, the smiles will return,
the sun will break out,
the music will play, and
you will finally be able to
move forward the life that
God intended for you
with grace, strength,
courage, and confidence.
Og Mandino

GRATITUDE AND COMPLETION

In the words of an old spiritual, "I ain't where I want to be, but thank you Lord I ain't where I used to be." More often than not, our lives shift in subtle ways that we may not notice on a day-to-day basis. However, when we review and reflect on the aspects of our lives that have changed and expanded over the course of a year, we notice that although we may not be exactly where we want to be, thankfully we're not where we used to be.

Making a gratitude list is a powerful spiritual practice and the perfect way to assess and learn from your year of "Spirit Is Calling." Take time to review your journal entries from this past year and notice the areas where you have grown in awareness and personal strength. Use the following pages to list the things that you are grateful for.

Gratitude List
MY HEALTH

List the things you are grateful for regarding your health. Include the people, situations, and things you appreciate that have contributed to your health this past year.

Gratitude List
MY RELATIONSHIPS

List the things you are grateful for regarding your relationships. Include the people, situations, and things you appreciate that have contributed to your relationships this past year.

Gratitude List
MY CAREER

List the things you are grateful for regarding your career. Include the people, situations, and things you appreciate that have contributed to your career this past year.

Gratitude List
MY SPIRITUAL GROWTH

List the things you are grateful for regarding your spiritual growth. Include the people, situations, and things you appreciate that have contributed to your spiritual growth this past year.

Gratitude List
MY FINANCES

List the things you are grateful for regarding your finances. Include the people, situations, and things you appreciate that have contributed to your finances this past year.